CONNECTING THE DOTS

THE COGNITIVELY CORRECT™ WAY TO SPEAK WITH PRESCHOOLERS

CARLA A. WOOLF

"Problems can never be solved at the same level of awareness that created them"
—Albert Einstein

ISBN: 978-0-615-14628-7

Library of Congress Control Number: 2007930495

Printed in the United States of America

In Memory of my Brother

Eric Alexander

Who always expressed
innovative ideas with a
Child's heart.

Thanks to all my family and friends-
you know who you are!

Thanks to the Horizon Diner and Rick's Café

PREFACE

EVER SINCE *POSITIVE DEVELOPMENT* made its debut on the scene of Early Education, and indeed in many fields of learning, it's been commonly referred to and defined as "Reinforcement."

Positive reinforcement has been in a class all its own experiencing an almost unprecedented popularity and fervor for prescribing "good" behavior. At the same time, though it possesses an allure, it is vague and its style remains obscure. Despite this deceptive void, it is eager to be captured and structured into a usable format.

Why has it eluded us for so long? Because, *Positive Development* has been confined and restricted to the single tactic of *reinforcement* as a sole formulary for implementing positive behavior expectations. Furthermore, the failure of "*reinforcement*" to produce a promise of positive behavior points to a missing link, its complementary component of **Enforcement**. In the interim, frustrated parent groups rally and organize to "turn back the clock" or re-implement the power of "no." Some even recommend spankings to enforce the type of dogmatic cooperation that earlier generations deemed proper and successful.

In earlier times, "Child development" was *enforced* with fear, and negative reinforcement. Today, Child development is *reinforced* with vague encouragement and <u>enforcement</u> suffers for a lack of definition.

Positive development is the combination of two active *forces* working together. Together constructive enforcement and positive reinforcement produce confidence, faith and self-esteem that cultivate, in children a "desire to do the right thing."

Children are naturally "good" like any seeds of nature that require proper care and cultivation. Left to chance, good children, like potentially productive seeds, may flourish or never flourish, can grow wild and out of control, produce a fruit or two and perhaps produce nothing. It's only common sense that anything being reinforced must first be enforced and anything being enforced can best be secured by reinforcing it. *Enforcement* and *reinforcement* are the *variables* that *yield* a complete and valuable *quotient* in the *equation* of <u>Positive</u> <u>Development</u>. Parents are children's first teachers and primary influence on their overall appropriate development. However, parents, teachers and other involved professionals must work together to ensure children's best development.

Most Early Education teacher-training demands some compliance about omitting the use of negative words and phrases that impair positive development. However, in many education facilities, it is left to individual teacher training. Furthermore, too many facilities are unfamiliar with the technique. That is a shame when you consider that all other teaching techniques in Early Education depend on the demand for this technique of positive constructive communication skills.

In the least, prospective teachers in training usually learn that the purpose behind implementing positive guidance is to support children's unrefined abilities for devising or "hypothesizing" acceptable options on their own. In other words, they are too young to possess and exercise the sophisticated critical thinking skills that are regularly necessary to make reasonable and constructive decisions. That is why, naturally, they need adult care, compassion and nurturing.

"CONNECTING THE DOTS" takes this understanding a step further. Human development is based on the process of **cognition**

– the ability to gain knowledge and use it, As such, a **cognitively-correct**^{tm} **process** for teaching warrants a **cognitively-correct**^{tm} *dialect* that parallels our innate and natural design for learning! These logical requisites call for the standards of positive language semantics to be acquired in the earliest stages of interaction and development.

How do we learn? Is there an underlying similarity or blueprint that drives our impulses? Do we all share a natural inclination to advance, achieve and experience fulfillment with respect to our individual and unique abilities? Are time-outs and threats truly acceptable tactics for imposing and demanding "good" behavior?

Is it normal or natural to learn through the knowledge of fear, guilt, consequences and mistrust? Or, is it more normal and *"desire-able"* to learn through the "knowledge of potential, trust, love and benefits"?

As we continue embarking upon a world consciousness, it is unfeasible for cultures, and interchangeably language, to remain stifled under the auspices of tradition that repel change or fear losing their identities. Without changes to our interactive language skills that express, empower and convey our intentions, we will continue to elude the vast amount of untapped potential we have and can conceive of achieving.

A superior consciousness demands the features and semantics of language to be filled with the knowledge of potential and possibilities, to entertain solutions that only a dialect - *free* of guilt, consequences and disadvantages - can offer.

We owe ourselves more than just self-improvement or how to **re-cognize** our personal beliefs and attitudes. Attitudes and beliefs should serve our talents rather than act as survival tactics that keep us from them. We owe it to ourselves and our descendants to cultivate a growing-up legacy that purposes true human potential from the onset of children's lives. That proposition is far more logical and productive than spending precious time and energy fixing what's broken inside of us, life after life and generation after generation.

Using positive words and phrases is more than just about being "nice". It's more than just the understanding that children are unable to guide themselves or that they have a right to choose. "Positive" in practical terms means we would be better off constructively exploring our talents and abilities rather than become experts on why and how things go wrong. Learning from our mistakes should be secondary to learning from our abilities. When we become experts on learning from our abilities, we will be better qualified to learn from our mistakes.

In order to extract the best of children's potentials in the formal years of education, a cognitively - correct™ approach for building intellectual knowledge will have rested profoundly on a cognitively - correct™ foundation of emotional knowledge and stability. Regardless of race, nationality, culture or gender, children deserve to receive the same qualities of appropriate cognitive development - a development filled with love, trust, and genuine encouragement to feel competent about their abilities.

Chances are this is a heartfelt desire and need shared by everyone who either has a Child, cares for a child, or who once upon a time was a Child. As you examine this "Dialect of Positivity", reach into your Childhood soul and see for yourself if these positive, logical phrases match your own original desires for guidance. Explore your own intuitive inclinations for the love and encouragement you would have wished for yourself as a Child – if you'd only had the power to exercise your own rights and privileges. In each of us still lives a Child – the real person we are and in so many cases, the person still holding the destinies we dared dream about as children.

Legacies can change us and we have the abilities, potential and talents to change them, let's take destiny into our hands – *Children of the universe* - "Unite!" – C. A. Woolf

CONTENTS

PART TWO

PART THREE

HOW TO READ THIS BOOK

"READ" MAY APPEAR TO be the operative word here, however in the context of this book, "how" is really the more functional term. Ideally, this manuscript, like any book or literary compilation, can and should be read from cover to cover.

This book is divided into three main sections and although they can be approached and read independently, they are distinct in such a way that their outlines are best comprehended in comparison with one another.

The *first section* defines the truthful elements that characterize positive preschool (3½ - 5 year olds) development. The theories and proposals follow titles and headings that breakdown the multi-diversified functions of cognitive development in the preschool stages of growth. This section is designed to point out that what we view as separate areas of development for preschoolers are in fact so closely related that they are virtually identical.

The semantics of appropriate communication with preschoolers demand omitting the use of negations. To demonstrate the possibilities of language usage according to the "knowledge of potential", this "dialect of positivity" is presented without the use of words such as no, not, don't, can't and shouldn't.

The *second section* is a *hypothetical* and *fictionalized* "interview" between two adults and one child. The young preschooler points out that most Childhoods have been fashioned around parent's expectations born of their own unfulfilled dreams and broken-hearted Childhoods.

The *third section* is a "language manual." Language and culture are identical, interactive expressions that represent a group of people. Language is the central steering system for directing cognitive abilities and the most powerful factor we possess for influencing human potential. Therefore, in order to acquire and achieve higher and deeper cognitive abilities, a culture must possess a Cognitively-Correct™ syntax that harmonizes with the basic design of human development and potential.

In other words, a Cognitively-Correct™ language supports the full strength of expression necessary to develop the aptitudes, motives and abilities that are naturally structured into every unique individual. Traditionally unchallenged commands – or cognitively-**in**correct commands – are "translated" in this section.

The goal of this "dialect"in part, is to examine and challenge the limited consciousness of civilization by diffusing the unpromising philosophy that we learn through the "knowledge of guilt, fear and consequences." This section is designed for acquiring and applying language skills that express the "knowledge of potential, benefits and possibilities" because that is how humans develop, grow, advance and prosper. It is an aspiration in practice and a contribution to civilization as we could imagine it according to our deepest desires and highest ideals.

It is an opportunity to recapture the civility of all great civilizations that have been conceived on the advantages and possibilities of human rights, talents and achievements.

A *grammatical* note from the author ~

As a matter of respect for the English language. It would be quite flattering to receive the praises of language experts such as William Strunk Jr. and E.B. White, authors of *"The Elements of Style"* or of Stephen King for his extraordinary account of *"On Writing – A Memoir of the Craft"* - both of which are two of my favorite "biblical" collections of English language rules and expression.

In lieu of perfect grammar and for the sake of recording a new dialect, I graciously and liberally (or viciously), relax and thank the flexibility of the English language and the historical documentation of Bill Bryson, author of *"The Mother Tongue – English and How It Got That Way" (Another testament of English,* A must read book*)*.

In the last two or three years of this eleven year project, I have depended on these resources for sane grammatical counsel. These gentlemen may beg to differ should they attempt to read my work here, and it makes me wildly curious to imagine how a writer such as *Jack Kerouac* would assess my alternative and unconventional vocabulary. Nevertheless I will cite Bill Bryson from "The Mother Tongue" (pages 141 – 142) only to quell what might be one of the most obvious violations of English. *"...enduring of Lowth's many beliefs was the conviction that sentences ought not to end with a preposition. But even he was not didactic about it. He recognized that ending a sentence with a preposition was idiomatic and common in both speech and informal writing. He suggested only that he thought it generally better and more graceful, not crucial, to place the preposition before its relative... Within a hundred years this had been converted from a piece of questionable advice into an immutable rule."*

There is still much to discover in the journey along the knowledge of potential and how culture and language will transform and shift in order to accommodate human advancement, or even how this book will be revised.

Having now put these ideas and premises in the open for debate, I beseech my readers to read into the nature and purpose of the "dialect" that resonates with the heart of aptitude and potential in preschoolers. It's difficult enough to speak without negations. The vital task here is to use language that reflects your heartfelt intentions for guiding your preschooler's abilities and discover how diversified elements of learning in this stage can influence the course of a lifetime.

Once children reach the Kindergarten/First Grade levels of development, their ability to reason with the rules and syntax of grammar can begin a regulation process alongside their gradual and increasing capacity to build hypothetical skills. And, may they learn the proper use of negations! By then, children's intuitively acquired "knowledge of potential" should be viably intact.

– The Author

PART ONE

I

MAKING SENSE

REAL CHILD DEVELOPMENT MUST be approached as a part of total human development. The processes of whole human development can only be addressed properly against the backdrop of Nature, taking into account the thread of inter-connected characteristics that run throughout every level of life. Societies may make demands about children's education and behavior, but just as a plant needs water and sunshine, children also require particular elements for growth.

Positive speech is the logical formula for communicating the intentions of good guidance. In practicing it, you will see for yourself how it matches your own intuitive inclinations for positive and constructive directions.

Altogether, the three main sections will lead you through the crucial importance and untold purpose of positive development. The entire text (aside from the cognitively - incorrect language examples) is a documentation for the possibilities of utilizing positive terminology without the use of negations.

Positive speech is a dialect. It matches our intentions for achievement, harmony, cooperation and the natural design of our productive inclinations. Moreover, it is a technique required to be used by teachers in Early Childhood education, and it is *the* technique for *all* other methods of teaching and disciplining.

The context of the technique breaks down conventional language and cultural concepts that have been accepted for too long as normal;

Concepts that have crept into our psyche without question and with little challenge.

Within the scope of these challenged ideas, you should discover that they bring you heart-to-heart with your Childhood, and your own original hopes and dreams.

Perhaps the joy of Childhood has eluded you. Perhaps you have forgotten your Childhood-self amidst experiences of confusion and shame. Perhaps memories of your Childhood innocence are revived. If you feel as though you can add conviction to the difference you would like to make in the lives of the children you love, or to yourself as an individual in the universe, then these pages will have spoken to you.

The idioms of positive speech can appeal to all endeavors in your life. Positive terminology will aid you in realizing your own intuitive awareness and all that is good in yourself. All of us have greater talents yet to discover and the ability to bring out the best in everything and everyone around us, especially children.

WHO ARE WE?

Desire probably best describes the motives and inclinations of human behavior. If the interconnected traits and intentions of desire exist within all of us, then there must be an original seed for that characteristic. Our bodies reproduce based on the program of chromosomes in our DNA patterns. Desire too, reproduces in a form of DNA. That would be mental, emotional and even spiritual DNA.

Unfortunately most cultures inherit and pass on false notions about human nature that are believed to be true or natural. These characteristics turn into legacies when they are replicated through language skills that make them acceptable. For the record, natural behavior is based on compassion and the <u>benefits</u> of living. Therefore language skills need to incorporate real human nature skills along with the possibilities for creative growth and advancement. Although individual traits of behavior differ remarkably, there is still little to distinguish our differences and compulsions for seeking and experiencing fulfillment.

These natural and original traits are vital elements that drive the forces of behavior or what may become the motives and tactics of our behavior when we are denied the very basic elements that perpetuate our feelings and purposes as creative beings.

THE INTENTIONS OF HUMAN BEHAVIOR

The early stages of development reveal a lot about human potential. There are profound advantages for learning to distinguish the differences between unrefined abilities masquerading as "poor behavior", innocent intentions appearing as bad motives, or cries for firm guidance materializing as blatant disrespect.

Real human, natural behavior begins with what we *can* do, what's in us, and what's "out there" to be matched with our own desires and abilities. By creating speech that is identical to the intentions we uphold for ourselves and the children we love, we can, in one fashion among others, begin to come to terms with real human potential.

JUST SUPPOSE..

Most of us follow some sort of belief system even if the choice for belief is to believe in nothing. Most everyone stands for, or stands by some idea, because we can and do think.

Traditional philosophies were designed to demystify ideas about forces of conflict that exist in life, or at least try to answer questions about conflict and attempt to provide solutions for creating peace, harmony and serenity. Still, others have proclaimed ideas that separate people as a race rather than bring them together. Such ideas often create exclusivity causing prejudice and derision toward anyone who refuses to comply with those ideals.

In nature, polarity and balance exist everywhere. The complementary, opposite counterparts of all levels of life, simple and complex, work together in the cycles of nature by instinct, devoid of external doctrinal influences. Nature projects a disposition of serenity and peace, without prejudice, to anyone within its presence. Nature has an aggressive side too, and although we are accustomed to regarding destructive feats of nature with contempt, we can observe that it is equal and unprejudiced in its demonstration of destruction to anyone in its presence.

If and when we take offense to nature's aggressive or destructive side, what does that say about us? Just because, we continue to make decisions such as building cities and ports where nature repeatedly presents its forces of destruction, while we challenge it because of our own ulterior motives, that hardly means we have reason to blame it. Where we harness its power, nature is usually content with complying, but where we deny or try to defy it, that can most likely be reduced to one thing – that we refuse to learn from its aggressive, destructive, or negative side of existence, power and potential.

Although nature is customized to create destructive forces, there are more constructive forces at work than destructive ones. Aggressive and destructive changes have made mountains, created lakes and rivers, and put dinosaurs to extinction in order to make way for other forms of life, such as ourselves. Unless we look at the positive side of nature's aggressive forces, or the balance of polarity that creates new forms of life, we may always be at a loss for understanding how we too progress. In nature, attributes of polarity or balance exist among all species; positive and negative, male and female. However, in our sector of life, we seem to view negativity as an end or conflicting force, rather than a complementary or contrasting force that works in conjunction with positivity.

Imagine then, as in the case of nature we might assume that negative and destructive are meant to be *catalysts* in the reshaping or re-construction of natural life and indeed of our own lives. Perhaps it is merely our aversion about negativity that has worked against us and we should derive clues from nature as to the catalytic force of negativity as mostly a constructive component. Rather than judge, condemn or try to annihilate it, we might re-view it as the natural missing link; a contrasting force of development.

If that holds any truth, perhaps we'd agree that we've misconstrued negativity's purpose by misjudging its potential, when it might be embraced as much as positivity. If we've allowed ourselves to be misled, maybe its time to put negativity into its proper order and classification as a contrasting and equally valuable component of positivity, as they are in fact, both needed for normal, functional progression. Before we define the true nature and potential of negativity we must explore our intentions to understand the true nature of positivity. Just as nature has produced a useful, resourceful world, we too must discover more of our own useful, resourceful abilities.

THEN WHY ELIMINATE "NEGATIVITY" FROM OUR COMMUNICATION SKILLS?

If negativity is really supposed to help us, then why the grand campaign to promote positive language semantics without the use of negations and negativity? It may feel natural or seem normal to hold nature or a supreme being in contempt of destructive forces, but how often do we hold ourselves in contempt of the destructive attitudes we maintain and recycle that are evident everyday in our speech, communication and interaction skills?

Are we out of balance with nature, because contrary to nature, we humans believe in destructive force more than constructive force? If we have managed to survive through our own destructive ways, then there must be a reason why we perpetuate. Why do we continue to settle for, or even cultivate ourselves for accepting life as if it naturally presents more disadvantages rather than advantages, impossibilities instead of possibilities? Do we, or should we raise children as if they were blank blueprints with a natural inclination leaning more toward potential malice instead of potential goodness? On which side do we each categorize our personal attitudes about life and human nature? Consider what the natural inclinations of our desires actually are as a review for defining our <u>real</u> tendencies. How can we explore changing attitudes that are reflected in our communication skills?

If it is at all a natural tendency for us to lean more toward malice, then why are laws designed to maintain goodness and order? Why do we promote and celebrate achievement? Why do we suffer from maladjustment? Most profoundly, why do we anticipate happiness and good fortune? Like nature, we *are* mostly good, why else would we tirelessly seek out goodness as a partnership in our lives despite the varying degrees of tragedies that constantly loom around us? Why do our language and speech patterns fail to honestly and genuinely reflect our good intentions? It's probably fair to say that we are inherently good, because goodness, simply and straightforwardly, is what we desire of ourselves and for ourselves.

If we actually had a clear, genuine and concise understanding about positivity, we would naturally understand negativity. The real reason why negativity continues to debilitate us is because we have eluded the true nature of positivity.

Nevertheless, for the sake of exploring and exposing all improper views about negativity and how it shades our understanding of genuine positivity, here, we will maintain the context of negativity's conventional definitions as we create a feast of positivity to reverse the way negativity has shaped our viewpoints. Where we have proposed or anticipated the probability of negative outcomes and undesirable consequences, we will stress definitive positivity as a barometer for defining the nature of the guidance we intend and the possibilities we can derive from communicating them appropriately.

THE QUEST FOR UNTAPPED POTENTIAL

The strategy for deterring negative words, terms and phrases as a method for standardizing true language expression should never be confused with its purpose and goal. It can hardly be a means within itself, because all language expressions have a message, and that includes the proper use of negations. The sheer purpose of positive terminology is to <u>give birth to ability</u>. It is to do away with the attitudes of inability that are deceptively hidden among the incessant use of negations and other negative expressions that dampen our aptitudes, creating an unconscious block between ourselves and our real abilities, or between our minds and our hearts.

It is a proposal for designing a new legacy of potential that begins with children's natural abilities and their right to inherit vital structures for learning, through the simple, positive, encouraging ways we speak <u>with</u> them.

WHERE DO WE COME FROM AND WHY ARE WE HERE?

Choose from any number of philosophies that appeal to you! There are however, systems of order we have some answers and understandings about that are virtually undeniable. In order to understand how we develop and how we can approach our best chances for improved potential, we need to have a basic understanding of how we are "wired".

II

IT'S A SIMPLE MATHEMATICAL EQUATION

EVERYTHING IN THE WORLD and universe; every function, every part of life, growth, existence and nature fall into some type of order, or patterns. The basic building blocks for all compositions depend on simple and complex patterns for their structure. That is especially significant and true, when you consider that the *particles* of all atoms are made of the same material and it is the *patterns* of atomic structures that constitute the distinction of particularly unique and separate elements. The mass of any atomic element depends on a repetitive replication of its own basic pattern to create its substance on a larger scale of matter. A tree, for example, follows an order of growth until it fulfills its destiny in becoming a tree. It may die before maturation, but it will never become anything else, such as an emerald or a whale. The pattern of its design is to become a tree and only a tree.

Cognition is the ability to gain knowledge. Knowledge is gained through the active use of all of our senses. We have two main types of intelligence; Emotional knowledge intelligence and Intellectual knowledge intelligence. If cognition is defined as acquiring knowledge - if knowledge is both intellectual and emotional, then, both types of intelligence are subject to the processes of cognition.

Is cognition logical and does it follow a pattern and sequence? If all structures for growth and development follow the order of patterns, let's explore what patterns and orders are and why they are necessary for all cognitive developments.

LET'S DO THE MATH

First, let's put patterns into a context or definition – what is a pattern actually? A pattern is the most fundamental form of math. *Math* in early learning is classified as *Cognitive Development.* Cognition is defined as the process of acquiring knowledge, so all starting points for knowledge are fundamentally mathematical because all classifications of knowledge are derived from basic patterns. Therefore, the cognitive process is itself is a mathematical function - able to process the sequence of patterns reflecting the structures of all elements and life forms that represent the basis for all knowledge. If learning is a logical sequential process that follows a pattern, it's only logical that we should consider cognition to be a logical process too.

DEFINING MATH – LOVE IT OR HATE IT ?!?

Do the math on any part of the universe and you will see patterns at work; basic elements in compounding variations that constitute different formations and structures that define their character and the logistics of every order. Some other basic fundamental math principles are sequences, fitting, sorting, classifying, identifying, connecting, measuring, guessing, reasoning, and after all that somewhere are ordinal and cardinal numbers that help us keep an account of patterns and orders. Learning numbers and learning to count have been gravely misunderstood as a basic math learning skill. Numbers, counting and calculations are arithmetic skills that in order to learn well, are strongly based on the broad range of the fundamental math principles, and for that matter, so are all other skills.

Why do so many people possess a fear or disdain of math? What an unusual phenomenon! Some people even have severe phobias about math and probably as many claim they lack an understanding about complex math. When you consider the fundamental structure of patterns as the basic building block for all life, growth and development, fears and misunderstandings about math equal a very odd paradox since we are a living, breathing, moving, thinking, feeling manifestations of patterns. We *are* a substantiation of patterns, or the basics of math, multiplied over and over again.

The patterns of knowledge are acquired and recorded by the receptors of our knowledge potentials – our brains and our emotions. Continuing knowledge development depends on previously acquired patterns of knowledge as predecessors for more complex knowledge acquisitions, such as in learning to count before learning to calculate. If we do indeed have two types of intelligence – intellectual and emotional, and if knowledge acquisition depends on patterns for information input, then both types of intelligence require cognitively-correct[tm] processes that match the design of our logically patterned structures.

Because patterns and numbers are infinite, we could infinitely hypothesize this premise from here until the endlessness of the universe, and from now until the endlessness of time. In any case, acquiring a literacy about basic math gives us an opportunity to treat math as a worthy ally, instead of an unworthy adversary. To align ourselves with basic math is to empower our understanding of its existence, purpose and usefulness in every part of life.

MAKING CONNECTIONS

What do children's development and human nature have to do with plain basic math, logistics or any other mathematical theories of relativity? Children's cognitive development is activated when guidance and education parallel the natural cognitive design of the brain and emotions.

In early cognitive development, the experiences of intellectual knowledge acquisition are still in the formulation stages, that is why preschool learning is classified as the formative years for development. But logical intellectual learning must follow or overlap logical emotional learning.

Acquiring and learning the skill for connecting separate pieces of knowledge can be defined as the ability to hypothesize (the ability to reason). Preschool children, generally lack this ability and therefore are unable to draw conclusions or make reasonable assumptions as a regular part of their daily lives.

Hypothesizing is an abstract and advanced cognitive skill. It is a math skill that can and should be used for all other skills. Our first learning skills are based in Emotional Intelligence. Children must first acquire the element of compassion that makes emotional learning logical. Before we become dedicated to making sure that children can read, write and count, we must make sure that children feel the patterns of dedication to their basic and emotional needs.

Children's impulses are clues to their potential talents. They must learn to feel, by adults' guidance, that there are reasonable outlets and activities for their impulses. They must learn first to feel secure about warranting constructive directions and feel accepted about their pure motives. Only then, can children develop a real basis for having compassion for others. The ability to use compassion means that we can view, sense and perceive the elements, aspects or position of someone or something. To do that objectively and fairly means knowing the value of something and what valued treatment feels like. (Most of the beliefs we uphold are either negative or inverted. In the case of compassion, we usually view it as realizing or feeling the acts of mistreatment and the inclination to offer assistance). However, the broader the perception of value, the broader the range for reasoning different compassionate possibilities for oneself and for others.

When we learn compassion we learn value, when we learn value we learn to sense qualities beneath the visible surface. It is a mathematical equation of "invisible numbers". It is the basis for learning to hypothesize. Fundamentally, hypothesizing is about making connections between things or ideas that are related or interconnected. Therefore, compassion, reasoning and hypothesizing are directly and indirectly connected. Receiving compassionate treatment makes sense to human design and desires. When we make logical connections in our emotional intelligence, we develop the ability to make connections in our intellectual intelligence.

Children do unconsciously and naturally, possess one sense of logic and reasoning. It is the love, trust and encouragement of their parents and caretakers. They simply and naturally rely on them for "good" and worthy guidance.

"Good" guidance then, must be prescribed by intentions and language that match natural cognitive development, reflecting the patterns of knowledge acquisition. The brain is designed to file information. The brain is unable to delete, negate or un-do information. Theoretically speaking, it repels negations or skips them, the same way computers do, it is designed to do, to receive - it is a receptor. So guidance and direction depends on a positive, constructive input for appropriate action.

III

FEELING VS. THINKING

W E LEARN TO FEEL before we learn to think. We have fallen into the belief that our brain does all of our reasoning, but the brain is subject to the commands of our emotions and motives, whatever they may be. Even when we attempt tasks or activities that are against our desires, it's natural to command the partnership of our wills for initiating action. Even in that case, only if we are accustomed to exercising our will. We can think forever, but unless we feel, we do nothing.

We do as adults, rely more on our brains for reasoning. Logically that should come as a natural inclination since our brains should have become fully developed by adulthood. Efforts and attempts toward self-improvement in adulthood are better realized when we understand the emotional cognitive processes that were thwarted in our own Childhoods. When our capabilities and feelings of competency are impinged upon by emotional disbeliefs and feelings of inadequacy, they are in fact illogical, especially when compared to the measure of designed potential we possess. We live by realities that reflect our emotionally acquired reasons for believing that the limitations we create are all we are entitled to have and deserve, but each of us possess what is needed to change that.

LOGICAL VS. ILLOGICAL

When knowledge acquisitions can congruently reflect one another emotionally and intellectually, then children can be fitted with a naturally intuitive ability to reason that will become fully accessible in adulthood. In other words, children must be in position to have inherited feelings of reason and logic while they begin acquiring thoughts of reason and logic.

When children's feelings and basic needs are criticized, denied, defiled or neglected, then their overall senses of *reason-ability* can be severely impaired. These impairments may show up in the immediate sequential stages of development, however most of the time they appear in the idiosyncratic behavior of adulthood; that time in life when we are expected to have the ability to hypothesize. How does that happen? Each intellectual process is supported by a counterpart of emotional knowledge. During the early stages of learning, each new intellectual concept or idea must make a "rite of passage" through a comparable attribute of Emotional Intelligence that receives and transports that type of sensory knowledge to the brain. If that emotional sense contains an illogical or damaged premise, then it mutates, inverts or contorts the receiving piece of knowledge which in turn, supplies the intellect according to the emotional assessment of that information.

The reasons and motives for thinking and acting are substantially established during the preschool stage when both intellectual and emotional experiences are fundamentally a singular function. As developmental stages progress past preschool, the attributes of emotion and intellect take on more independent functions. The characteristics of each contain the quotients of knowledge they were originally built on, affecting a lifetime of decisions and interactions.

In the case of intelligence vs. ignorance, when pieces of emotional knowledge are damaged, then it is only natural to develop a sense of fear for particular subjects or ideas. The misappropriation of knowledge will support circumstances or strong opinions that induce ignorant fears, such as in, "I hate math."

Fears that preserve our safety and are supported by our instincts are certainly natural. However, fear that would be used as a knowledge quotient will only function as a characteristic of ignorance. Fear blocks us from exploring possible traits of truth and patterns of elements pertinent to whatever premises we might intend to acknowledge.

POLARITY WITHIN US.

The grand mastery of academic education is widely accepted as the path to success. But there are many folks who live abundantly and successfully without formal education. Many folks live according to the inclinations of their natural abilities and aptitudes, or at least try their best to do so despite challenging circumstances in life. In lay terms, we consider these folks as those who follow their hearts and passions.

Emotional Intelligence (or "**E.Q.**" = confidence, healthy self-esteem, competence in work and creative projects, caliber of social interaction, ability to be intimate, ability to discipline talents and potentials, be compassionate and feel love), *is the driving force and motive for the application of accumulated knowledge and the unique qualities of* **Intellectual Intelligence** (or "**I.Q.**" = intellectual knowledge, skill improvement and precision, trade experience or academic achievement, use of critical thinking skills/deductive reasoning, memory, and communication), *all of which depend on normal E.Q. functions.*

IDENTIFYING OURSELVES

Unique talents and abilities are the strokes of individual identification. We are embodiments of will and creativity. The sooner we organize changes that fulfill the disciplinary needs of the varying talents of individuals the sooner schools can be classified as universal institutions that offer equal education.

If we continue to rely only on intellectual intelligence as the gladiator of leadership, or as the sole provider of solutions for human advancement, we will continue missing out on the possible contributions that can be made by each and every citizen's valuable and diverse abilities.

As democratic as we strive to be, the only way to propose "desireable" responsibility is to ensure the freedom and advancement of individual talent value, because it is competent citizens who make up a competent society; <u>Never</u> the other way around.

We are creative human beings. In order to feel emotionally fulfilled, we need to create based on our own abilities. The more time, effort and energy we spend creating constructively, the less we could feasibly spend on being destructive, thereby identifying ourselves with the balance of constructive forces in the natural world, our home.

We are all on the short end of the stick when it comes to emotional, mental, spiritual and even physical care. If cognitive development were sufficiently activated in any of us, especially in our emotional faculties, we could find ourselves at a more substantial crossroad of advancing human development and active brain power. The qualities and requisites for normal, happy and appropriate development are the birthrights and entitlements of all children and the Child that still lives in each of our souls.

LIVING IN THE PAST, LIVING IN THE FUTURE

How much do we really learn from History's mistakes? Where is the balance between learning about the unfortunate circumstances and consequences of the past vs. learning how to emulate decent plans and measures for implementing beneficial changes? Are we partial to knowledge about what is wrong and what has gone wrong, just because there is so much more of it to learn about? Is it any wonder why we keep repeating history, and the mistakes we are so familiar with? As a common cliché goes, whatever it is you focus on, is exactly what you will extract.

Without understanding how traditions of behavior are molded into legacies and without focusing on the changes we intend to make, we are already destined to recycle our current human development notions and issues into upcoming generations. For every incident or feeling of pain, shame, guilt or incompetence that "grown-ups" re-live, there are direct connections to our Childhood lives. These impressive experiences have set in motion the dispositions for re-enacting similar emotions. They cultivate the nature of the tasks and activities we are inclined to pursue, and the reasons behind them.

Every time we hesitate or deny the realization of our own aspirations as adults, we might assume proportionally, that somewhere there is a Child reduced to feeling ashamed about pursuing their own naturally good impulses and pure motives. When children want to explore their own environment but feel limited about discovering their natural inclinations, they begin diminishing their desires - the substance of their own future potentials.

As each generation makes claims to desire and emphasize greater achievement for their own children, a possibility for significant improvement may be attained when a legacy proposed by a dialect of achievement is cultivated and transpired by an entire race of people who all desire to feel fulfilled and accomplished. A culture of positive language semantics can transcend differences while a connection for fulfillment is reflected in a dialect that speaks from our hearts.

SPEAKING TO OTHERS AS A NATURAL REFLEX OF HOW WE'VE LEARNED TO SPEAK WITH OURSELVES.

You can also say that we've learned to speak to ourselves based on the way we've been spoken to. The main parts of speech in any language are verbs and nouns and the pronouns that qualify them. The other main parts of speech; adjectives and adverbs, modify the main parts of speech. Verbs describe the actions we intend to perform while nouns represent the objects we intend to attain, realize and experience.

Whether you consider yourself a leader or a follower, sooner or later, you will run into the obligation of making decisions for yourself, which *will* require you to be your *own* leader. We all have a will, and it is meant to be used. Whatever language semantics and attitudes you're accustomed to using for your internal self-speech, will directly or indirectly be reflected in your decisions. Likewise, decisions we make, because we are obliged to do so whether for better or for worse, can change the way we think or feel about ourselves and the circumstances around us.

If we spend more time and effort dispensing directions with negations and then wonder why children are unimpressed with a single positive direction, then it is we who should be impressed with the negative conditioning we have taught them to abide by. Try as we may to disengage from the power of influence, it is a fruitless effort. Children learn attitudes the same way they learn speech and habits from their parents.

Parents are children's most important teachers. We can utilize many sources and options to gain I.Q. (Intellectual Intelligence). However, there are only two possibilities for gaining E.Q. (Emotional Intelligence) - you receive it from your parents in the developmental years, when the brain is forming. Or, you can give it to yourself as an adult.

Do you remember the saying "Sticks and stones may break your bones but names will never hurt me". Intuitively, we understood that to be false, The truer saying should be: "Sticks and stones may break my bones but words will definitely hurt me". The truth is that words are harder and deadlier stones than actual tossed rocks. Harsh words and stone hearted opinions from others hit us softly when, we have been guarded by our parents' trust, support and encouragement of our personal abilities that give us a "Rock of Gibraltar" security.

IV

RESPONSIBLE FREEDOM

ALL ENTITIES CONTAIN ATTRIBUTES of duality and form additional functions with complementary counterparts that balance or complete them. There are a few elements in our natural world that are independent or "inert" and lack the need or purpose to seek a counterpart (or to complete the structure of their outer atomic orbits, because they are complete). However, most basic elements are compelled to seek a relationship with other elements in order to fulfill or develop a new or separate function during which the basic characteristics of each merge or change.

Similar to nature, most qualitative "elements" in our lives are compelled to seek an additional element or quality to complete a more functionary purpose. It is rare in nature when something is the result of one element or cause and so it is the same for our ways of life. For responsibility, that complementary element is freedom and vice versa. Realistically speaking, responsibility and freedom would be dysfunctional without one another. Responsibility involves making choices and choices require having freedom. Unless the freedom to make choices is available, then responsibility is nothing less than mindless commands and unless freedom is upheld by responsibility, it would lack sensibility.

Freedom is often wrongly defined as; experiencing or feeling the lack of responsibility, being able to pursue desires without the need, conscience or obligation to fulfill other tasks and/or being considerate of others. Like many notions of human interaction and development, we stand to lose a lot when we misunderstand the anatomy of our real nature. As human beings, our nature compels us to have desires, feelings and attitudes. They are the underlying reasons for fulfilling responsibilities.

Although an individual's attitude <u>may</u> be indicative of how they approach responsibility, it is never any person's right to judge another person's feelings or attitudes, and least of all in the area of responsibility. Nevertheless, it is an individual's obligation to himself, to maintain the freedom of making choices by honoring whatever the "responsible thing" is to do. However, individuals are "free" to feel, think and have an opinion about the issues and situations around them regardless of the nature or level of their responsibility. In plain or derogatory language – if you want to have a bad attitude or any other attitude – that is your business and your business alone, and it <u>is</u> your personal right. That is a harsh way of saying that we are each free to retain ownership of our own attitudes, because we are able to design them by the use of free will.

However, it is with regard to responsibility that people receive the most judgement and criticism. This is a rather convoluted process in human dynamics and relationships. Why? Because either culturally or conventionally we believe that personal feelings about responsibility must be determined by the person dispensing the responsibility. The usual expectation is that unless someone maintains a noble or feelingless attitude about fulfilling a responsibility, we find it permissible and even acceptable to assume that, either their work ethic or personal character is of poor quality. In technical terms it is virtually impossible to convey the process of responsibility without simultaneously explaining Emotional Cognition, Emotional Ownership, Critical Thinking Skills and all the functions of preschool Development in the same breath (more about these in the sections to follow).

As adults, every task we do involves some act of responsibility, from how we eat to how we tackle global challenges. So taking care of things or being responsible means processing a full sense or awareness of our feelings that represent the things we care for or own. Rebellion then emerges (usually in the later stages) when we have surmised a sense to refuse that we must adopt others' feelings or assessments regarding the fulfillment of our own responsibilities. Our feelings then are what make us own our responsibilities. This general misappropriated version of how responsibility works is the most deceptive practice of mixed emotional ownership and is therefore the most characteristic of the knowledge of guilt and mistrust than any other areas of human interaction.

Children adopt good feelings and attitudes about responsibilities because adults encourage and praise them for <u>fulfilling</u> them, regardless of their mood or attitude while they are doing them. Imagine that! <u>Fulfillment</u> works for responsibility as much as it works for our talents and happiness! If you have encouraged your children to fulfill a responsibility and they comply, your responsibility is complete for that situation. If they comply with a grumpy attitude, that's fine and it is unnecessary to tamper with their efforts. If you decide to tread into the territory of judging their feelings or attitudes when you have already generated their aptitude, you are obstructing two very important lessons. Firstly, feelings should be respected, and if you disrespect children's feelings, what lesson do you think you are teaching them? Secondly, they would miss the opportunity to experience fulfilling an act of responsibility in spite of their feelings or moods, and what can be a more invaluable lesson than that?! – it's what we tell children life is made of.

It is the parents and caretakers responsibility to supervise children's activities and encourage them through the acts of responsible behavior and responsible care for their playing environment. Learning responsibility is a continuing process and children need consistent encouragement and specific positive directions that appeal to their abilities. Although you may find yourself reiterating "the rules" over and over again, children need the security of knowing that guidance will always be both in front and behind them so that they can enjoy the freedom of playing; which will become the freedom of working and ultimately the freedom of taking responsibility.

WHOSE TERMS ARE WHO'S?

Children's potentials are like unopened gifts that are pre-packaged, waiting for you to discover and for your children to explore. You get orange juice from squeezing an orange, and coconut milk from cracking open a coconut, and you'll never squeeze blood from a stone. If you try to change the package contents, you will run into problems in the unfolding and unwrapping process. If your Child is fascinated with textures, playing with mud pies, finger-painting, or building blocks, chances are he'll be happier in design, art, cooking or architecture than he would in the board room or as an accountant. Where you observe children who are constantly banging out rhythms, singing, bent on listening to music incessantly, imitating adults, dressing-up, role-playing, or talking and asking questions every waking moment, chances are they are a potential musician, entertainer, psychiatrist or philosopher. If they like taking things apart and putting them back together, they probably possess some kind of technical abilities.

Unconditional acceptance is part of the underlying process of trusting and understanding children's respective abilities. Children should never be treated as auxiliary vessels for the specific purpose of fulfilling anyone else's dreams and aspirations. Any imposition unto a Child from others to be someone or something in particular against the grain of their natural and creative abilities can only be defined as conditional acceptance of who they are. Such dynamics constitute the acts of conditional love instead of unconditional love.

BLAME VS. RESPONSIBILITY

Blame and responsibility may give the appearance of being interchangeable traits, but they are diametrically different. Functionally they are totally separate and incomparable. They produce conflicting effects and rarely ever produce contrasting or complementary effects. That is to say that, rather than moving toward constructive solution and order, as would be in the case of responsibility, with blame you are moving in totally the opposite direction.

If children were born with an automatic pilot to be perfectly decisive and responsible, it would be justifiable and customary to blame them for every act of irresponsibility. Blame is too often used to point out a lack of responsibility. But, blame lacks order altogether and therefore lacks a pattern or formula that can be logically fitted into cognitive abilities, whether intellectual or emotional. Blame can only be reduced to uselessness in human development. Blame contradicts how we learn and develop. We are designed as all nature is; for usefulness.

Knowledge is acquired by all dimensions of our sensory perceptions. Our first knowledge acquisitions are acquired by our emotional perceptions. So, when we arrive at adulthood, whenever we use our intellect, there is always some kind of original emotional charge behind it. We may believe we are just thinking, but there is always a motive behind our thoughts. If blame is repetitively used as a disciplinary measure to learn, we can become stricken by the notion that we must be shamed into learning, or that learning must be based in the knowledge of guilt and consequences.

The purpose of stressing the cognitively-correct^{tm} approach in preschool development is because it is the only stage of development where imagination is still in "full bloom" and the stage where all functional foundations for intellectual capabilities can be introduced. These learning processes are at the most impressive stage for being emotionally charged and motivated because E.Q. and I.Q. have identical characteristics.

Imagination is the lining of all learning functions which are rooted in Emotional Intelligence. When shame is added to the feelings of learning responsibility, it impairs learning functions including imagination which is the key to intuitive learning.

Responsibility is best learned for its benefits. We are beings driven by desire, so we should learn the desirable attributes of pursuing life's tasks and activities. Anything that is learned primarily by its consequences leaves little desire to pursue it (be it responsibility or otherwise).

Children's natural motives and inclinations are innocent and pure. They are compelled to explore the world around them that is constantly beckoning their senses. We are designed to learn through the knowledge of potential, benefits, advantages and constructive possibilities.

Taking responsibility means taking control (ownership) of our own feelings and abilities. In childhood, we must be given the elements and qualities that allow us to feel competent about responsibility. When potential has been damaged in childhood by guilt, judgement and blame, it naturally carries on into the subsequent stages and eventually into adulthood. Responsibility should become a natural response to our abilities.

Blame makes it impossible for us to make free and responsible choices for our own lives. The freedom of the knowledge of potential must be activated and fostered in early Development to give children the best opportunities for fulfillment. When we are halted by feelings of blame and guilt, we fuel feelings of inadequacy and suffocate the intuitive inclinations that can help us to connect with our own genuine potentials. That is to say that, rather than follow our own personal feelings, we would have to be constantly wired into someone else's feelings. To find the clues to our personal potential, we need to look to our own natural inclinations and desires.

Why are the characteristics of imagination, knowledge and responsibility placed so heavily in the context and realm of preschool development? It is only the preschool stage that encompasses the unique uniformity of all learning functions. In light of this realization, all authorities involved at this stage of your child's life must also work uniformly to ensure appropriate development. In realizing that this stage has direct ties to the subsequent stages of growth, it is unfortunate that it has received the least amount of credibility about its influence over a lifetime of issues and development. The psychological, social, literary, mathematical, physical and spiritual functions of preschoolers are one in the same. Therefore, the formula and method for meeting challenges and designing curriculum according to natural development should also be that way. In the course of exploring and discovering total human potential, the preschool stage holds many clues; there are cognitive developments that happen only during this stage. It is, in the better interest of personal livelihood, to formulate constructive purpose from the onset of one's life than to adjust behavior based on symptoms that appear in the subsequent years and stages of development. In practical terms, it becomes triple the work with half the results.

TRANSFORMATION

In the pursuit of advancing potential, progressive changes can only be made in stages, because a total turnover of life and society is unrealistic and impractical . We have to start from the inside, and the best place to start is with each new individual of a new generation.

We are subject to the times, environment and conditions of our societies. Parents are busy working hard to provide a decent living for their families. Real progressive changes are best made with preventive measures. Our general knowledge quotients and the language we use to express our knowledge must transform from the knowledge of guilt and consequences to a knowledge of potential and advantages. One of the first steps in changing the emotional legacies of disorderly expression is to withhold projecting feelings of guilt onto your children when for instance, leaving them behind day after day. When we tell children the reasons for our obligations that credit and console our own personal feelings, we inadvertently implore them to consider our feelings and forget theirs. Children are unable to extend understanding and compassion for adult's obligations. In examining the source of guilt, you may want to explore how your own parents, however unintentionally did the same to you, whether it happened through illness, death, financial stress or neglect. When adults expect compassion but fail to extend it, it is usually because when they were children, they were expected to dismiss their own feelings of sorrow. That is how the knowledge of guilt is learned and passed on generation after generation.

The world of emotion is visually concrete for children, they will pick up on whatever feelings you have. Their only choice in these scenarios is to surrender. Surrendering means giving up what little control they have (about expressing their feelings) and replacing it with insecurity. When children are unjustifiably blamed for their naturally justified feelings of loss and separation, they can and probably will acquire the detrimental "naturalness" of guilt. Instead, at least, give all of your children's feelings equal and valuable credit by offering *your* full compassion. Their feelings should be fully accepted by giving proper recognition and *names* to each and every emotion without blame, guilt or the expectation that they should understand adult's priorities and schedules. (A cognitively-correct[tm] example: "I feel sad when I'm without you too. You're allowed to be mad at me for bringing you here while I work instead of being with you. I'm sorry it has been that way. I understand if you want to cry, but I hope you have a fun-filled day. I love you, here's a big hug for you. So long.")

This emotionally literate statement gives children the freedom to own their true feelings, without giving them up. In other words, it is unnecessary to feel "guilty" (relinquish ownership) of their feelings. For the child, they'll feel they can entrust the feelings of their heart to their parents. For parents, this will allow them to continue an emotionally intelligent curriculum of security, confidence and trust that children can only get from their parents.

Children learn through exploration and discovery. Through those processes, they can experience and witness the patterns of production and what they equal. Children experience all of the same emotions we do. If children feel blamed, criticized, accused or judged for feeling a particular way, then how can we possibly help them become educated or literate about productive options for their feelings and impulses. The primary and first acquisitions of knowledge require us to experience and own our emotions, but if we are required by guilt to give up an emotion, then we lose opportunities for discovering and processing them. All emotions, when dealt with constructively, give power to the potential of our intellectual capabilities.

Emotional intelligence provides us with the literacy to identify, learn and explore what each and every emotion is. Blocking our emotions literally clogs the passageway for creative impulses to flow freely. Creativity fuels a continuing desire for a lifetime of learning.

DEFINING LANGUAGE

Why are verbs the main parts of speech? Because we are productive, creative creatures, who have created verbs to actualize our intentions to produce and create.

So if the main bulk of our languages are verbs, and if language is probably our most concrete influence on potential, then why is the bulk of our potential lurking in limbo?

By the time children are 6 years old, they will have heard the words; *no, not, don't, can't and shouldn't,* 3-5 times as much as all other verbs combined in their native tongue and that is probably a conservative calculation. Why de-power verbs, why do we delete action words with negations when there are plenty of verbs that describe exactly what we mean to describe?

Once the preschool stage of development ends and the next cognitive stage begins (usually when they understand the difference between fantasy and reality), then children can learn the proper use of negations. In the meantime, children should learn the proper use of language in general. The first language we use is classified as our mother tongue and the one we use to express our thoughts and feelings. Children should understand, they should *feel* - through their E.Q.'s and imaginations - that all things are possible, that all things <u>can</u> be done and we should speak and teach a language that reflects endless possibilities. Luckily, for all of us, we are designed to continually acquire abundant knowledge and the ability to learn new languages.

In order to transform the patterns of inhibitions and negative beliefs or attitudes that are taught by reckless verbal-negations promoting a language of mistrust and impossibilities, an inversion must take place. By listening to ourselves communicate ***cognitively-correct*** *tm **virtues*** for guidance and achievement, we match our own intentions to guide with positivity and even diffuse some of the shame and heartache acquired from cognitively-incorrect guidance from our own childhoods. Positive **verb**-alization constitutes a constructive and formidable means for pursuing and fulfilling purposeful, virtuous actions.

MATCHING COMMUNICATION AND
ACTION WITH INTENTIONS TO "GUIDE"

By learning a dialect of possibilities within our own language that is congruent to the idioms of potential, we can change the way we cultivate behavior and the behavior of ability will manifest according to the good intentions of human aptitude. In this attempt to re-structure our language patterns with positive "speech-ability", we can re-create a pipeline of development that transforms an unconscious language of <u>inability</u> to a conscious language of <u>ability</u>.

DIVERSIFICATION

Since all forms of life, growth and development depend on patterns as building blocks, and (a) patterns define the fundamental structure of math, then all (b) learning categories are also subject to (c)basic mathematical principles (if a = b and b = c than a = c). Preschool math is defined as cognitive development and it is by this principle that all subject matters are one in the same for preschoolers. (Refer/review section "Let's Do the Math".) All subjects are interconnected and overlapping in a way that makes them indistinguishable – because they are all fundamentally mathematical (patterns). Therefore any one subject must be introduced by including as many diversified learning functions as possible. Doing so presents a process for children to explore and to discover the patterns or mathematical structures of different subjects even in a single, but diversified activity. Children could care less about the subject classification of any given activity. As far as they are concerned, if it's appealing to their senses, then that's what counts. The more senses you include, the better!

By making such methods available in open-ended free play activities, or by implementing them in hands-on lessons, children's learning experiences can be saturated with exploration that introduces them to patterns, and the qualities of interconnecting traits - Be those lessons in a school or home environment.

Eventually, this intuitively acquired "connection skill" emerges in adulthood by naturally combining Emotional Intelligence (the lack of fear or guilt for natural abilities) and Intellectual Intelligence (the ability to see patterns in all subjects). This complement works purposefully without the strain of illogical premises. (Which are sadly solidified in the <u>formative</u> years of Emotional Intelligence).

EMOTIONAL COGNITION/ INTELLIGENCE

How often have you witnessed an adult making the most foolish of decisions when beneficial or advantageous options are right in front of them? Or wondered how someone came to the most illogical of conclusions when common sense is the obvious choice?

Intelligence in modern society, is generally recognized and accepted by the measure of <u>intellectual</u> facts accumulated in the brain or in memory, and the capability for its reuse. However emotional intelligence has the capability for reuse as well.

There is such a thing as emotional logic! Although we have been accustomed to believing that emotions lack rationale, emotional intelligence like all other parts of life, are subject to the characteristics of logical cognition. (Or, the acquisition of pattens for gaining knowledge.) Emotional reactions lack logic and rationale because they are based on a lack of emotional literacy and knowledge.

Emotional intelligence however, is still subject to ignorant judgment because its value is only beginning to gain credibility in formal education even in the most advanced societies. Where many changes are occurring for "politically-correct" reasons, based on research and social progression, there is still a long way to go to implement "cognitively-correct[tm]" changes – changes that combine both intellectual and emotional learning as equally valuable qualities that are necessary for appropriate development. (Versions of elective education measured by timed tests limit our perceptions about the diverse facets of intellectual intelligence. Nevertheless educational institutions are designed around a system of testing, while totally failing to identify any of our emotional intelligence skills which contain our motives for action.)

EMOTIONAL OWNERSHIP

I.Q.'s and E.Q.'s must be connected functions. The ability to <u>think</u> is based on the ability to <u>feel</u>. Severe differences in that relationship can create gaps or breaks that are never fully recoverable. As an analogy, imagine I.Q. and E.Q., each as one of the parallel and connected rods of a DNA molecule, representing the formation and basic structure of human nature and cognitive development. Now imagine breaks in those rods – much the same way you would realize how a physical composition would be damaged by irregular or malformed DNA (or chromosomes that have some kind of weakness or defect).

What does this have to do with emotional ownership? Well-functioning, critical-thinking skills require the union of intellectual and emotional quotients. It is activated through the process of connecting facts along with imagination as the catalyst to determine all new possibilities. The most saturated stage of learning through imagination is present during the preschool stage of development. Therefore critical thinking needs to be fostered during a stage where I.Q. and E.Q. are functionally identical. (In other words, the chromosomes of our emotional DNA and the chromosomes of our intellectual DNA must perpetuate in a complementary pattern or formation. Together they compose a function that activates our natural aptitudes.) Although, real critical thinking skills are used in adulthood, its foundation is conceived in the stage of learning through imaginative possibilities. When we restrict preschool learning to; classroom style settings, workbooks with singular formularies, or dispense discipline with negations, we indirectly and unwittingly judge children's imaginations. When we judge their imaginations, we judge their abilities by creating limitations for learning - where imagination has none.

When children are cultivated to receive guidance by a language of inability (although unaware intellectually), they become emotionally inclined to anticipate the negative guidance as "familiar logic".

Through the familiar "routine" of negative guidance, children create an order of security where they begin to understand what is "expected" of them. Children require guidance that can be customized to match their naturally pure and innocent motives. What makes it virtually impossible for children to devise their own constructive alternatives for activities and behavior? They must be able to hypothesize. However, hypotheses require knowing truthful factual premises and children are <u>ruled</u> by imagination which exceeds truth or logic.

Children need to be "strung along" so to speak, with their imaginations and good motives intact and instructed with positively-able options and activities availed with diversification to parallel their naturally pure motives, to explore and discover.

Imagination is the foundation of all learning in preschool; reality, fantasy, EQ, IQ, and the freedom to explore and discover the tactics of responsibility are all connected by imaginative learning. These functions are inseparable. To have personal feelings and imagination suppressed or denied is to do the same to all other functions of learning.

Current wisdom proposes that when children reach for items that are off-limits or react to people and circumstances with manners that are inappropriate, then they should be separated from the act or reaction. From that point they can be guided appropriately. This appropriate guidance should omit criticism and the temptation to judge children as bad simply because they <u>did</u> something wrong. However, this process is too demanding, because it is extremely difficult for children to change their attention on command (explained further in the sections titled "Applying positive enforcement with positive terminology" and "Putting Distraction to Good Use".)

The philosophy of communicating the knowledge of potential promotes more than just trying to reason with children about wrong-doings or that an adult can patronize them with *love-ability* even though they have strayed from good behavior. Cognitively-Correct™ language captures children's innocent intentions to explore and learn, by prescribing activities, toys or others materials that immediately remedy the innocent impulsive inclinations of their unique but unrefined capabilities. By immediately re-constructing the activity (without the interruption of negative criticism and shame), this allows children to keep their imagination and brain activity flowing in a cognitively-correct[tm] fashion of learning and development.

There will be times and stages throughout life for children to learn other purposes and how to practice hypothesizing through them. It's important for now, for children to understand that their purposes are their own. They need to gain trust and confidence in their abilities and the pleasure that is derived from that process. Whatever children are engaged in, it's impossible to know for sure how their imagination is involved, but you can be sure it is. When the flow of imagination is disturbed for the sake of criticism, it disrupts the flow of learning, and it can sustain severe damage if its flow is interrupted to imbue the details of consequences and disadvantages. That can diminish their ability to make connections which is the foundation for learning to hypothesize.

How do parents and caretakers transform a legacy of guilt, inability and personal childhood heartache into a new legacy of potential, trust, love and competence? As stated earlier, all elements naturally seek complimentary unions to fulfill a new function or purpose. A dual function must also be sought in order to secure the continuity of legacies that procure the destinies we anticipate for our children and ourselves. The knowledge of guilt and fear have been deceptively cultivated through language skills which debilitate human potential. Language is felt emotionally long before it is understood intellectually. In a reversal of cognitively-incorrect emotional development, or for the re-seizing of emotional ownership, a new legacy of communication must be established. Parents and caretakers can experience for themselves the vindicating effects of language communicated by cognitively-correct[tm] virtues of development.

Knowledge is acquired by all of our senses. Acquiring new knowledge, means re-employing our sensory abilities to develop new beliefs. By recruiting our own voice and subjecting our own ears to the requirements of cognitively-correct[tm] directions for teaching and disciplining children - adults can begin to intuitively recollect memories of guilt and the suppression of their own abilities denounced in their childhoods. As adults, we allow the quiet voice in our heads to haunt us with the pain and heartaches of our past. In other words, it becomes unnecessary to use our learning senses for reiterating what we have already learned and now believe. It has become "common" knowledge to us and it suffices to circulate it in our own minds without consulting our intuition or basic instincts.

By utilizing cognitively-correct[tm] communication, adults can engage in a memory and recognition process of their own childhood, re-cognizing that what they desired of their parents and what they deserved as children was the correct instinct and that being reduced to shame and confusion was the incorrect feeling to have.

Guilt, acquired by judgment, **requires us to relinquish ownership of our own feelings and hand them over to someone else's assessment and demands for action.** The cognitive process of emotional intelligence endorses the logic that we can fulfill tasks and responsibilities because we own the feelings behind them, so we want to do them. Without full ownership of our own feelings, we are forced into developing a false sense of responsibility that includes others priorities often at the exclusion of our own, instead of a genuine feeling that compels us to follow our hearts.

Once the knowledge of guilt is acquired it becomes a triple-edged sword. It slices through self-confidence, it captures situations and relationships that demand self-sacrifice and the worst cut of all - the self-imposed guilt for having the audacity to re-claim ownership of one's own feelings, desires and aspirations. In any event, taking responsibility means taking back and re-owning feelings about personal abilities and destinies without the guilty feeling that we are obliged to satisfy others' ideas and feelings while dismissing our own. When we acquire the knowledge of potential through the rights of emotional ownership in the formative years, we can instead avoid the exhausting work of finding ourselves and our talents later on in life (which are contained in our passions, feelings and inclinations).

When we are in a position to be confident, wise, fulfilled and emotionally intelligent, then we are in a better position to give to others, and able to nurture the children we love, who will have children in the future to love and nurture.

EMOTIONAL COGNITION AS THE FOUNDATION FOR CRITICAL THINKING SKILLS AND THE ABILITY TO HYPOTHESIZE

As previously stated, there are only two options on the journey of Emotional Intelligence, either it has to come from our parents while we are growing and developing, or we give it to ourselves in adulthood. Either way, we must acknowledge that ownership of emotional intelligence is personal. Once the stages of growth are completed, we are in a better position to take control of our own desires and free will. Thus giving ourselves the ability to manage challenges, or if need be change our fate and circumstances.

Parenthood is based on the joy of love and fulfillment, although it also paired with personal sacrifice. Parents should feel secure and satisfied with their growth, maturity and having experienced the passage of a (joyful) childhood. The less of a childhood a person experiences, the harder it will be to parent, but it can still be done.

In order for a legacy of emotional cognition to develop according to real potential and human design, children's needs must be fulfilled by *fulfilled parents* or parents who are willing to meet the requirements for cognitive development.

Plenty of dedicated professionals work tirelessly to create awareness for appropriate development. However, there are several misconceptions about early educational development and the standards of appropriate curriculum requisites for preschoolers.

Many of these requirements for early education are overlooked in order to appease the pressures of competition and higher education, or the preparation for them. As the pressure for academic excellence rises, the compulsions to fine-tune academic skills ripples down into the earlier years of education and has even reached down as far as Kindergarten and preschool. The precedence for filling these academic factors means that appropriate early education curriculum skills are replaced with close-ended lessons instead of open-ended free-play activities.

The detrimental factors that are evoked by this procedure causes deficiencies in areas that will affect a lifetime of developmental necessities. Cognitive development is subject to a sequence of stages which have to happen in order. There are certain <u>foundations</u> of development that occur **only** during the preschool stage that will ensure appropriate cognitive development. Two of these skills are Creative development and Critical Thinking skills. Creative development contributes to talent refinement which is necessary for self-fulfillment. Critical Thinking Skills contribute to the abilities of hypothesis and reasoning. These processes give an individual the power to make reasonable and responsible decisions, better known as common sense (or the confidence to follow their intuition and instincts).

Both common sense and creativity rely heavily on the ability to connect diversified pieces of knowledge. Let us examine: the process, the importance and the calculation of these skills. As children move past preschool development, their cognitive abilities take on the more sophisticated math skill of classification. This new stage makes it easier for children to understand the distinct characteristics and separate qualities of different subjects and elements (such as in the difference between reality and fantasy.) In preschool all characteristics and functions of development reflect similar or identical qualities of knowledge and learning.

Common sense and critical thinking skills, that go hand in hand, command the ability to connect or combine separate and interchangeable qualities of knowledge, whether they are concrete or abstract. (Although an adult may be unaware, when hypothesizing, he or she is intuitively subscribed to an earlier cognitive stage where all learning functions were overlapping and intertwined as one.) The only real difference between common sense and critical thinking skills is that common sense is about using already familiar connections of information that have become second nature (example, the trash goes in the trash can). Critical thinking skills are based on the already acquired reflex of putting facts together while exploring and applying, (the option of) adding new information for problem-solving, for developing innovative ideas (example; let's compact the trash), or to improve personal intuition abilities.

However, when children are consistently required to learn through close-ended methods that demand the correct answers they risk losing certain cognitive developments. Diversified learning means involving as many senses as possible including movement. The more different senses are involved in learning, the more different dimensions of the brain will develop. There is a very thin line for preschoolers between learning classroom style and just sitting in front of the T.V. Anything less than diversified learning is an inadvertent judgement on children's abilities to learn through movement, exploration and open- ended activities where all answers and possibilities are correct. For this stage, E.Q. and I.Q. partner together as identical functions and imagination takes on its most hardy role. The three become a trinity, inseparable and unbreakable.

During this preschool stage of development, knowledge acquisitions must be free of guilt. If guilt, fear, mistrust and consequences are used as a primary method for teaching, then that foundational temperament will permeate every process of learning and future knowledge re-use. Once guilt is imbedded in the singular process of interconnected preschool learning, it becomes grafted onto other functions where eventually they will have begun dividing into separate categories of knowledge. When children reach the following stages of education, each classification of learning becomes reduced to learning through shame (or restricted from the exploration process). In other words it will become a normal process to learn primarily through consequences, guilt and disadvantages. Once the preschool stage has passed, and the damage has been done, there is little that can be done to recover it, there are only managing techniques which we can employ to rectify it.

Why does this process stay with us? We carry guilt, shame and confusion into adulthood because we have acquired its knowledge during a stage when we are unable to reason, foresee (or hypothesize) that, one day we would be able to trust our own instincts and abilities. During that stage we still completely trust those who care for us and love us. Nature designed our survival to be dependant on our parents, what else are we to do - we believe them!

Let's consider critical thinking skills as being the final quotient of particular variables calculating human cognitive development or to reason our purposes for living. Each person possesses the capacity for critical thinking to design their own life as they choose. Who would freely give that power over to someone else? Who really wants to be at the mercy of others for devising and implementing options, possibilities, opportunities and solutions for our own personal lives when we each possess the capacity to do that for ourselves?

Critical thinking is the central sensory system of maturity, responsibility, intelligence, decision - making and in practical everyday living - sanity (contemplating the possibilities of our existence). Now calculate the congruency of these elements in relation to total development or extended brain capacity.

As a general premise, consider these ratios to hypothesize the theory about language and its influence on our potential. The brain only files, retains and processes active instructions or commands for immediate or future action. The brain is, however, subject to our sense and feelings of competency (self-esteem and confidence - trust in our own abilities), which is filed in our emotional intelligence.

We learn through our senses. When guidance and directions are dispensed with negations, the negation has to go somewhere, it is just a natural law. Since the brain is unable to file negations, it rejects it. Where does it go? It (the negation) gets stored into the emotional intelligence.

Why do we use so little of our brain or intellectual potential? It is because, it is weighed down by the feelings of incompetency. If we calculate the percentage of verbs we use with negations, it is quite possible that we would be examining a direct proportion between how little intelligence we utilize and how much negative language we use to de-construct our motives for action. The brain is inclined to process actions - verbs that define the knowledge of what we <u>can</u> do - acquired through all our senses. The knowledge or feelings of inability then, are learned in the emotional intelligence (since the brain only files what <u>can</u> be done). The <u>lack</u> of potential-knowledge-use is learned and acquired through the overwhelming stock of negativity (negation to verb ratio), causing a dysfunction or disunity between the emotions and the brain. As we have already examined in some detail, activating and utilizing potential is a combination of E.Q. and I.Q.

Appropriately developed emotional cognition depends on feeling the distinct and sole ownership of personal emotions and passions that constitute the nature of our own talents and aptitudes. So if we are to think about how to best use our talents, we must first learn to feel our own talents. That is our best criteria for developing critical thinking skills and creativity.

Personal talents initially show up in the most unrefined fashions. The last thing anyone needs, least of all children, is for their best abilities to be suppressed, denied, or judged in the name of good behavior. Where and when was it ever engraved in stone that the consequences and disadvantages of anything must be learned before and above all possible advantages and benefits? Since when were we all made to feel guilty about wanting to learn through pleasure, confidence and all the desirable possibilities of fulfillment?

For all of us, our talents should initially be recognized and encouraged by the unconditional love we receive from our parents. How can we begin practicing unconditional love? Is it by giving children everything they want and ask for? It is by accepting unconditionally - <u>their</u> talents and abilities. Unconditional love may seem like an unattainable ideal. But unconditional acceptance is a perfectly feasible approach.

The cognitive process of learning is the same for all individuals. By funneling constructive positive directions into children's abilities, parents or caretakers can customize guidance and unconditional love to address each unique child.

Through language we should have learned to cultivate ourselves to feel and think of our feelings and thoughts as our own. Critical thinking skills are impossible to have (own) if we lend them or relinquish them to others for control. Through cognitively-correct™ language we can re-cultivate our speaking, thinking and feeling skills to match our natural design for learning and fulfilling our abilities.

The training ground for exploratory learning requires the use of imagination and the freedom to discover patterns. Discovering and exploring patterns will lay a foundation for exercising common sense and critical thinking skills thus completing a cycle of learning to hypothesize in the future. When we are in the stage of unconditionally trusting in the formative years and are forced to surrender our feelings and impulses - imagination goes with it because it is attached to our abilities and so it shrivels up the seed of critical thinking skills.

When children are constantly denied the opportunities to engage their natural inclinations, if they are misguided or neglected, life seems to make very little sense. They have been thrown out of rhythm with the Nature of themselves. They will always see themselves and the world with an askew point of view that restricts their sense of possibilities, solutions and choices.

Sophisticated hypothesizing means having the ability to foresee possibilities. It means being able to abstractly envision the connection between causes and results, or the differences between benefits and consequences. True hypothesizing includes the sense to realize how decisions and conclusions will affect others. How will the world <u>be</u> a hundred years from now if upcoming generations are raised on the ability to truly hypothesize and practice critical thinking skills? Imagine someone who imagines - without restrictions, without guilt, blame, inhibitions or resentments; what kind of compassionate solutions to the world's problems will they devise?

V

"ATTENTION PLEASE!"

W E ALL DESIRE AND require attention and we'll probably never escape being emotional and social creatures. The type of attention and recognition children pursue is indicative of the type they become accustomed to receiving. Interestingly, the adults in their lives also become accustomed to recycling that same type of attention.

The more attention and credit you give to appropriate impulses and actions the more you will create a desire in your Child to receive that type of attention. If you are going to create an imbalance anywhere, this is the area to do it - give a lot more credit and attention for appropriate actions and very little credit and attention for inappropriate actions. Intercepting (where needed), offering positive direction and assuming children's good motives will develop and create a desire to behave well, creating the setting to continually dispense healthy attention . It is a mathematical equation in progress - it is a cognitively-correct™ process.

PUTTING DISTRACTION TO GOOD USE

While it is popular and effective to distract a toddler from an inappropriate object or activity by presenting them with something else, it is a worthless tactic for preschoolers. Distraction takes a different turn in this stage of development. Trying to distract a preschooler in the midst of an action is patronizing to them. They can outsmart that tactic by now.

Children's deeds and actions should only be judged according to their presumably well-intended motives (i.e. assume their motive is good). It's tempting to judge the motive according to the action, but kids are natural explorers and masters of imagination. You may assume what *your* best intentions would be, were you in the same situation. In other words, where preschoolers are concerned, you must distract them by keeping their motive and imagination intact, while instructing them into re-arranging their activities or impulses. Question their actions with the assumption that they were intending to do something honorable. (Ex: *" I know you like to help me in the garden, but this is my garden. You can only touch it when I am working on it. Let's buy you some of your own seeds so you can plant you own garden next to mine. Right now, you will have to help me re-arrange and fix the misplaced plants. I appreciate your desire to help but growing plants need to be kept undisturbed in the soil. You can learn that, by taking care of your own garden."* - Make sure you have positively enforced the rules about your garden or any other off-limits areas.)

Once children are verbally rewarded and encouraged about their most noble motives and potential abilities, you can instruct them through the steps toward an activity that matches their good impulses for playing, learning and discovering. Children are impressionable and they will see themselves as you see them. They will adopt whatever impressions you bestow upon them. String them along the lines of their imaginations by pointing them toward another constructive activity. They will rely on the same encouraging affirmations from you for each new activity. This pattern will be set in their emotional "mind". They will experience constructive use of their abilities and you will experience a more harmonious and cooperative atmosphere.

APPLYING POSITIVE ENFORCEMENT WITH POSITIVE TERMINOLOGY

How does positive terminology change the consciousness and development in children, and for that matter, in the rest of us?

Fundamentally, positive vocabulary gives substantial power and meaning to the core concept of "Positive Development". It gives children's potentials and abilities the time, quality and credibility that negative guidance or direction will ultimately impair.

It is common sense that anything needing reinforcement, must have certainly been enforced first and anything being enforced is best secured by reinforcing it. Preparing children with specific positive directions first, gives you the power and opportunity to reinforce your expectations should their actions go awry. Keep in mind that the best way to propose cooperative behavior and enjoyable activities is to focus your disciplinary efforts primarily on enforcement and secondarily on reinforcement.

Relying on "reinforcement" alone can be counteractive in developing children's sense of self-control and responsibility. Such guidance can be vague and confusing to children because it falls short of enforcing and guiding their actions when they would be involved in activities or before they would engage in them.

Children need guidance that helps them feel empowered, with a sense of competency that comes from within themselves - as opposed to feeling presided over by fear or harsh demands that force children's compliance and cooperation. Behavior commands that are regularly dispensed with fear have negligible positive effects. More likely, it can cause deeply-rooted feelings of rejection and mistrust. Although it conventionally accepted to instill fragments of fear to avoid dangerous elements or to prompt reactions in cautious situations, it is always better to endorse cooperation through trust and confident competency. People of all ages and in all types of situations overcome and defy fear everyday for all kinds of reasons. It's far more worthy to bank on trust and competency even in fearful or dangerous situations than it is to depend on fear. Fear's presence is unpredictable. It may be helpful or it may be debilitating. Competency is more predictable and therefore more dependable.

Children at this age can never be put in a position to wait and worry about the assessment of their actions. Their emotional literacy is the basis for all subsequent knowledge. Discomforting situations and challenges must be addressed immediately otherwise anxiety or confusion will brew in-between their action and your guidance. We are all designed with a sense of moral fortitude. We may believe that children <u>know</u> the difference between right and wrong. However, they actually only <u>feel</u> the differences between right and wrong because they are still equipped with the pure emotional visibility to recognize goodness. It is a totally different function than hypothesizing right and wrong as adults do. It is natural for them to anticipate good guidance and compassionate encouragement because they want to feel valued and capable of doing well and doing what is right.

Children's impulses, feelings and attractions change from moment to moment. It's stating the obvious, but it is difficult to keep up with them and anticipate every more they will make. This is why enforcement and addressing children at the start of activities is vital to a harmonious and cooperative setting.

When children stray from appropriate activities or behavior, they need to be addressed and re-directed immediately. Dispensing threats and consequences is a poor method of discipline because it lacks direction. That is why it is cognitively-incorrect. If you wait to discipline or re-instruct a child, it causes confusion because they are always in the moment, so to speak.

Delayed discipline only amounts to shame in the child's heart and nothing in their mind. It is impractical because it requires a child to construct an abstract bridge in their mind between how you would have expected them to feel during the time of wrong-doing and how they feel at that very moment of your disciplinary advice. That requires a hypothesis, and as we have already examined in detail, preschoolers are just beginning to gather the tools that will help them learn to hypothesize in later stages of development.

VI

WHAT IS POSITIVE DEVELOPMENT?

THIS MANUSCRIPT IS CONSTRUCTED with the intention of proposing a prototype for Positive Terminology. The lists of phrases are designed as "positive translations" for negative, vague directions that leave children feeling confused and ashamed, shattering their self-esteem.

The word "confidence" originating from Latin is the same as the word "trust". Although we have come to understand the two words with distinctively different meanings, their original definitions implied the same meanings. In applying that to children's development, trust and confidence function indistinguishably and inseparably, yielding a foundation for faith. Faith is a by-product of love, trust and confidence.

Developing faith should be part of the emotional cognitive and emotional ownership process. It is prevalent and societally or culturally proposed that faith can be acquired later on by exterior, philosophical doctrines. But that is also a cognitively incorrect process because faith requires owning our own feelings of confidence. If we have missed the opportunities to own our own confidence in the early stages of cognitive development (mainly preschool development because that is where all functions are one and the same), our feelings of faith will be superficial or compelled by the knowledge of guilt.

Real faith requires us to feel and think for ourselves. Faith is probably the most abstract of emotional knowledge developments. Faith implies belief. Children must learn to genuinely <u>believe in themselves</u> confidently, by their own abilities, so that they may naturally believe in and trust others.

In early development, faith's seed is planted when children believe that you believe in them. They acquire this belief because you provide them with activities that help their abilities to flourish. Additionally, they receive confirmation for their efforts when you have expressed your own confidence, trust and faith in their developing abilities. Even if their performance falls really short of fulfilling a task competently, they will have believed and imagined they have done it well. They will feel compelled to continually seek out a vote of confidence, whereby you can reiterate, time and again, the fantastic job they did the last time. By doing that you will put them in a position to faithfully receive more precise guidance to improve their skills with each new activity or event. (Thus, fostering the desire to do things right and to do well.)

When you direct children verbally through activities with active instructions that reflect your "positively" good intentions, they can witness and acquire "faith" by tasks done with their own hands and of their own volition. They will develop the qualities of emotional and intellectual confidence, creating a united intelligence acquired through the use of personally owned learning tools: the senses.

Real Positive Development speaks to the ability within the Child. It's true purpose is to incorporate a design for learning that fits the blueprint of human cognitive potential - the ability to acquire knowledge. Language is the best resource we have for circulating knowledge and influencing potential.

In order to properly acquire knowledge we must use a form of communication that parallels the emotion's and brain's activity structures for processing and using knowledge. It must address both quotients of knowledge, emotional and intellectual, which are subject to the logical processes of cognition (learning through the senses). That form of communication is the cognitively-correct^{tm} system of speech, the only way to achieve the true knowledge for potential.

VII

TRUST MAKES THE
WORLD GO ROUND

WHAT IS THE SUBSTANCE of all things abstract? What is trust, love or imagination made of? What are the mechanics behind them and what is their energy source? How do they operate and why do we need them?

It's time to cease the madness about babies and children arriving at the doorstep without any instruction booklets. It's true - it's unnecessary to understand the mechanics of everything you operate - such as your car or laptop computer. But children are procreated beings, as we are, who will one day be adults. And each one will grow up retaining a child that goes on living in their soul just as we have. The instructions for growing and living are written inside each and every one of us. We should know the mechanics of our souls because they house our desires and desires compel us to make conscious, willful efforts to pursue what we desire.

All the things we desire to attain in life are useless without love. And love is pretty useless and dysfunctional without trust. Why are babies born with a natural disposition to trust unconditionally? Because they are predisposed by design to be loved unconditionally and children trust that they will be loved by their parents.

So how is trust dispensed to children? In preschool development children continue learning the lessons of trust stemming from compassion (their inherent sense of value) when they are encouraged to care for their possessions and environment with a similar sense of value that they have acquired in their own emotional intelligence so far. Children must learn responsibility with regards to their own purposes and priorities, before they learn other (outside) responsibilities. Creativity and imagination play important roles in the trust and responsibility functions of development because trust and responsibility are also based on personal aptitudes and talents. The order of learning functions jumble in varying sequences, whatever children are doing, but they are all there beneath the surface. Therefore, if children are guided constructively or assumed to be able to use any or all functions to tackle a task, they feel trusted to utilize their capabilities. When they are guided to use their own hands and other learning senses, they feel accepted and free to exercise their unique talents.

Trust is the basis for all relationships and that includes the relationships we each develop with our own personal abilities. We all possess a natural sense of vulnerability. When we trust ourselves, we allow our vulnerability to be led by our confidence - substantiated by our developed talents and abilities. (Because, ideally we acquire trust in our E.Q.'s by our parents' unconditional acceptance of our capabilities - the structured portal of unconditional love). The superficial powers of mistrust, incompetence, fear and rejection impinge on our ability to trust and believe in ourselves even in spite of natural aptitudes that are built into every human being. A lack of confidence - the lack of trust in ourselves due to undeveloped abilities, (originated by conditional acceptance/ conditional love), cause the delicate internal attribute of vulnerability to surrender to mistrust and rejection. (That is why neglected or abused children grow up struggling with responsibility, or self worth, or relationships, or work, or all of these).

Having confidence in ourselves means trusting our own abilities. In adulthood, this should feel natural and should have a coordinating effect within ourselves and our ability to create common bases with others and their abilities. But if we reach adulthood with the anxiety and preoccupation of managing our own confidence and trust, it extracts too much of the emotional energy we could be using to further develop the personal talents and abilities we do have - abilities that are either dormant or undiscovered. It is far more demanding and requires a willful sense of self-intervention to become actively involved with a pursuit to develop self-confidence and self-trust. By adulthood, we should have been, at least, pointed in that direction when we were children. Nevertheless, we all recognize that ideally, it would have been better to have recieved guidance and support to encourage self confidence and self trust from the start - but it is never too late to pursue your talents and passions (and therefore develop or recapture your own sense of confidence).

In our own lives as children, we have very little control over how much our parents would have extended trust to us by the time we will have reached adulthood. The same goes for when they had been children and so the cycle continues. How much any parent trusts in a Child's capabilities is usually directly proportionate to how much they had received trust for their own capabilities. In spite of that, when we are grown, when we can take back ownership of our own feelings and thoughts, talents and capabilities (to trust ourselves) - we can re-invent ourselves. However late it seems, we can explore our own talents and learn to confide and trust in ourselves.

Trust is already a natural and active part of our daily survival. We trust that we will stay grounded by gravity. We trust that the earth will rotate around the Sun and never get close enough to burn us or too far away to freeze us. We trust that there will be air to breathe and water to drink. We trust that nature will flourish and keep us secure on this planet, (if we let it). We trust that there will always be people around to make life interesting and worth living.

The practice of cognitively-correct[tm] development - what you surmise intuitively, is what can be done. Pass that tradition onto the next generation and you will begin to change the legacy of limited human development that has plagued civilization for generations.

Preschoolers can do practically anything adults can do. Even with limited resources, children can be entertained around the house with common household items or by just trotting around the kitchen table. As they naturally explore and find things to do, (aside from activities that carry a health or safety risk) they can discover the connecting qualities of the immediate environment that is familiar to them. To do that much you will make them feel trusted, responsible, and competent enough to tackle their respective personal abilities.

ENFORCEMENT VS. REINFORCEMENT

If it is your intention to guide children to the best of their abilities, then that guidance must be positively based on their natural tendencies, impulses and potentials.

If the sole purpose of your rearing obligations is to ensure that children understand the negative consequences of undone tasks, then you will teach your children how to miss opportunities. But, if you continually show your children the benefits of getting the tasks done, you will instill the joy of advantages for taking on "obligations". Leave natural consequences to themselves as much as possible. If you are spending more of your time giving positive and constructive direction to your children, ultimately they'll figure out some practical concerns for themselves. The same can be said for your current life situation right now. If you only focus on negatives there will be little room for the possibilities. Acquiring a wealth of literacy for consequences and disadvantages will only create a depressive and oppressive lifestyle. Get busy learning the joys and benefits of life and teach your children to do the same.

"Positive Reinforcement" - the catch phrase used in most Early Education handbooks, is a Single Element in search of its complementary partner. "Positive Reinforcement" on its own is a lone variable in an incomplete equation. It is inadequate, unbalanced and makes consistent positive results difficult to yield without constant cajoling and frustration. It must be balanced by its complementary variable. One that supports a consistent desired outcome. The equally important variable is "Positive Enforcement".

As a mathematical equation, it would resemble as follows:

| *Intentions* | + | *Words and Guidance* | = | *Appropriate* |
| *to Guide* | | *that Reflect Intentions* | | *Development* |

OR;

Confidence & Trust	+	*Enforcement of Rules*	=	*Reinforcement*
Specific Positive		*Observation of*		*Desired*
Guidance		*Natural Skills*		*Outcome*

THE 5 STEPS OF POSITIVE DEVELOPMENT:

1) Eliminate the use of negations, negative words and phrases, (such as no, not, don't, can't and shouldn't).

2) Implement the use of enforcement with specific, constructive directions about what children <u>can</u> do, and are permitted to do.

3) Use Cognitively - Correct[tm] language that parallels the natural design of the brain to acquire knowledge that endorses the feelings of competence in the emotional intelligence quotient.

4) Acquire and utilize the Knowledge of Potential as the true purpose of Positive Development by speaking to the abilities within the Child - addressing the diversified possibilities of learning.

5) Use Reinforcement as a confirmation of what has been done correctly to create children's habit to seek out "good" attention, establishing a desire to do what's good and right. Reiterating with positive, constructive language the improvements that need to be made.

VIII

MATCHING OUR DESIGN
FOR USEFULNESS

THE REQUISITES FOR GUIDANCE and teaching preschool children begin with a dialect of possibilities. This manuscript uses a side-by-side comparison of conventionally common statements, commands and topics of conversation as **cognitively-correct**[tm] phrases (vs. cognitively - incorrect phrases) designed for practical use.

A Positive Dialect: the first step for sanctioning positive and cooperative results with regards to teaching and disciplining children. A lifetime of positive attitudes and trust in their own abilities begins with eliminating the use of negative and debilitating words and phrases such as: no, not, don't, can't, and shouldn't.

CHILDREN'S OPINIONS VS. PARENT'S DECISIONS

A campaign for positive development must authenticate a few clear concepts. To begin with, children's development requires parental level decision-making power. Firm discipline should include teaching appropriate responsibility, guidance and provisions for constructive diversified activities, safety concerns and the dispensation of empathetic and positive encouragement. At the same time, children need to feel confident about expressing their thoughts, feelings and personal preferences, because like everyone else, they have them.

Learning to listen to children is just as important as speaking to them.

To help children feel included with their opinions, parents may indulge them to offer their viewpoint about certain activities. All too often, parents make it a practice of seeking counsel from children about everything, especially important or serious family matters. This creates a sense of role reversal that can undermine a Child's sense of security, and thus weakens the parental level of decision making power. Children also lack sufficient maturity to carry the burden of expressing an opinion for every event that is to ensue, they are already too preoccupied with their own "jobs".

CHOICES VS. ALTERNATIVES

The theme of positive development has been muddled by promotions of offering choices and worse, confined to the back-order of "reinforcement" which has already been discussed in some detail. The philosophy that, "You always have a choice", has somehow trickled down into little minds that lack the ability to reason but are packed with absolute determination, leaving parents in some very defenseless situations. It is easy to believe that children devise this tactic on their own.

Why do we use consequences threateningly if we want children to understand the joy of making choices and taking responsibility? Is it any wonder why we have unconsciously attributed negative humdrum to so many choices and responsibilities we are obliged to fulfill?

If, or when we force children to follow through on their responsibilities with "or else" as a threat, it falls a bit short of the appeal to do either. So, what are the choices? Willful children may choose the consequence just so that they feel they have a choice in the matter, and the opportunity to exercise some control.

The best petition here is to use the modifying parts of language to the best of our knowledge and educational experience. We've created adjectives and adverbs with good reason too. If we expect children to realize the meanings of specific words, sophisticated or otherwise, we have to put them to good use.

The proposal here then is to specify the difference between choices and alternatives. Children need to be given alternatives that they can process, right then and there as an incentive to fulfill their responsibilities. By telling a Child his teeth will fall out if he chooses to forfeit brushing is a little too abstract for them to comprehend. If you use threatening consequences on your own terms to impose certain submission, remember they are good at imitating and you could find yourself on the receiving end of the same tactic.

Propose <u>alternatives</u>; brush sitting down or while listening to their favorite music. If they enjoy hard candy or pizza, they are better off with healthy strong teeth to chew it – that's a concrete choice. To introduce children to the concept of choices, they can be applied to other scenarios that are nonobligatory, such as deciding to go to the park or elsewhere, or deciding to do nothing at all.

Alternatively, we can choose the manner and attitude in which we handle the choices we make. In general, choices may be defined as decisions we must make, exercising our will to fulfill them, and alternatives are about using our creative devices to work through those decisions.

POSITIVE VS. NEGATIVE

It may seem that developing an environment of positivity must be indicative of all smiling faces and the lack of confrontation that would threaten the balance of a happy positive atmosphere. Real positive development deals with the combination of I.Q. and E.Q., as equal temperaments that align our motives and ideas for action without conflict. Any issues of conflict, confusion or anxiety that are forcibly suppressed in the name of a positive atmosphere will inevitably cause deep feelings of negativity that eventually will seek some form of release. The longer the conflicts are in a suppressed state, the more negative they become. They should be dealt with in a positive confrontational manner.

Unfortunately, the shift toward creating positive attitudes has falsely conjured the misunderstanding that all confrontation would be negative and therefore should be avoided in order to retain peace and positivity. The only way to inhibit the expansion of negativity is to nurture seeds of positivity that diffuse the effects of negative feelings which cause repetitive negative behavior. Once these negative behaviors surface it is very important to unleash the conflict that results in undesirable behavior. The core and cause of an issue is what should be confronted, and confronted constructively, by promoting positivity from the <u>inside</u> out.

As adults we may schedule speaking about an issue with another adult, but in all stages of Child development, even through the teen years, issues must be addressed as they arise. Scheduling emotional stability for your Child is never the best option.

It is sadly a rare occasion to observe constructive confrontation among two or more adults, and children, too often, witness this. In a typical scenario, a discussion pursues. One person, wants to address an issue, the other wants to avoid it. This usually results in one calling the other "argumentative" while insisting to "let it go" as the only proposed resolution. (For the record, an argument is when two or more people *are* trying to resolve an issue but neither side can agree or compromise on the solution.) More commonly, if and when a discussion is pursued, the distressing emotions resulting from the unresolved issue become the argument itself. In such a case the issue stays unresolved and produces more negative feelings that will be recycled in the next disagreement. Constructive criticism breaks down the issues to be amended with positive options and alternatives to be implemented. Destructive criticism breaks down the *person* by judging their personal feelings and evading the issue.

We are so accustomed to dealing with the symptoms and distress factors of an issue, rather than resolving the issue itself that causes the symptoms of distress. Why? Because we are cultivated to recognize and credit disadvantages and negative implications far more than ever recognizing benefits and advantageous resolutions.

When our language semantics can transform from the knowledge and literacy of negativity to a literal knowledge of benefits and constructive opportunities, we will be more attuned to creating solutions that resolve challenges and disagreements. Whenever possible adults should discuss disputes in private. But if the discussion is so urgent or necessary, the best example adults can set is a productive discussion of advantageous options and zero insults.

IX

POSITIVITY AS A FORM
OF LITERACY

HOW OFTEN DO WE stop and think about properly translating our words to reflect our truest intentions? We are often so unaware of the quality of our communication because we are accustomed to believing it is a natural way to communicate and express ourselves. One of those "customs" is the blind-sided belief that having good intentions are sufficient coverage for positive counsel. An example of that would be how we unconsciously bundle and repeat good-meaning advice such as; "Did you know that is so bad for your health", as opposed to saying "Did you know the benefits of changing or eliminating that habit are..." Is it any wonder why we resort to the same negative habits when our acquisitions of knowledge are based predominantly on what is wrong and what is bad?

Most adults acquire new knowledge through reading. Historically, even literature has its base in cognitively incorrect terminology highlighting the negative of life instead of the positive. Literacy covers many forms of reading. The most fundamental characteristic of reading is association. When we read symbols, words, trails or expressions, we associate or assign particular meanings that have been designated to those symbols. We use many different forms of literacy to gain knowledge. If the symbols and expressions we use for communicating and learning about thoughts, feelings and ideas fail to match the intention, or intended meaning, then there is literally, a quantum breakdown in the equation of communication from feeling - to thought - to word - to action.

In review, cognition is defined by the process of absorbing or acquiring knowledge through the exploration and experience of our senses. Knowledge is stored into our intelligence files. We have two main types of intelligence; emotional and intellectual. Re-**cognition** or recognition can be defined as the re-use of acquired knowledge, applying meanings we've learned and experienced to communicate and express ourselves with associated symbols we've agreed upon.

Even when we express our dislike or displeasure, it should express our exact thoughts and feelings. When we acquire a literal confidence in our communication skills, we would find ourselves feeling less offended of others feelings and opinions. (Because we'd possess a confidence to own our own feelings and opinions while respecting others rights to own theirs.)

For the brain to use all of its cognitive potential, it is conveniently wired and designed for recording the *ability* of actions. If emotional intelligence is warped with judgment, guilt and criticism, you will warp the creative use of intellectual capabilities. (Because we think based on what we feel). If we wish to expand our capabilities, then we need to acquire a dialect that expresses the unlimited possibilities of our desires, which are the seeds of our talents and creativity.

Imagination is a characteristic shared by both our intellectual and emotional intelligence abilities. Imagination is free of time and space limitations. It is designed to accommodate ideas and abstract concepts beyond three-dimensional conditions or matter – which means it can be imprinted with just about anything.

We may outgrow a lot of our imagination, but it is a characteristic we still share with children. Begin associating children with good motives and good abilities and their imagination will do the rest of the work. It is essential to separate and disassociate children from their inappropriate actions. When children are judged or constantly reprimanded according to their misdeeds, they in essence lose their esteem as they begin to view themselves as the critical act itself.

So why would we address one another, or guide children with negative commands in the pursuit of gaining positive knowledge? Literacy begins with association. Begin associating children with good motives and they will develop a literacy of positive attitudes.

Our mother tongue is the naturalized dialect we use to speak to ourselves internally. As adults, we should continue to grow mentally, emotionally and spiritually, even though we have outgrown the stages of development.

Positive cognition is based on possibilities. Humans are designed to do, and to create. Growth, development and change can only occur when we are willing to do what we <u>can</u> improve on, rather than what we should just <u>stop</u> doing. It is all about action.

Positive literacy should enhance lifetime skills for continual learning, help build healthy self-esteem, self-confidence, competence, compassion and consideration for others to acquire the same for themselves.

MORE ABOUT EXPLORATION AND DISCOVERY AS THE FOUNDATIONS FOR ALL LEARNING

Time consumed with memorization, reading, flash cards and writing takes away from time that children would spend exploring and discovering. Time that if used to play and imagine, allows children opportunities for learning about our diversified world through all of their senses. Children's early learning experiences depend on the use of all senses, especially their hands, eyes, audio, movement and taste senses.

As previously explained, all functional areas of learning for preschoolers are one in the same, or indistinguishable as any one subject. Restricting learning to a particular subject or method is detrimental to their appropriate cognitive development because they are going to be inclined to explore anyway and inhibiting them is going to cause feelings of shame and confusion for following their natural impulses. Activities that involve free exploration and discovery provide clues and opportunities for you to observe children's natural talents so that they can be fostered and developed. Your emotional attitude of acceptance toward their particular talents and abilities help them develop a connection to their talents while they are acquiring intellectual knowledge and evolving as independent users of that knowledge and their abilities.

Innovation is part of the purpose of any disciplinary field and it relies on the freedom to explore outside of conventional ideas. Innovation is the ability to make connections of acquired facts and relative information by re-creating them as new concepts or for a new purpose. Innovation requires the use of intuitive abilities. Intuition is the ability to see the connections between elements that on the surface seem characteristically separate.

Trying to derive new ideas from stringent, and unchangeable concepts makes creative, open-ended exploration impossible and is uncharacteristic of imaginative possibilities. If innovation is the remedy for staleness and stagnation, then intuition should be a regular and natural part of creative thinking and development.

For intuitive intelligence functions to develop, children's learning environments should be equipped with a diversification of toys and activities. As children create and develop their bonds to different activities and functions that feel like one thread of learning topics to them, they intuitively learn about the connections between separate ideas and entities. Later, when sophisticated learning abilities enable children to separate and categorize different subjects, there will have been original connecting features, because once upon a time, they were all one.

Even if you disbelieve in intuitive awareness or intuitive intelligence, you should be able to connect concrete ideas together that are in fact, connected. The ability to reason and make wise decisions depend on connecting related variables – better known as critical thinking skills or learning to think logically and reasonably for yourself– to fulfill a task or attempt to create solutions for a challenge at hand.

Playing is children's job and their job contract should include spending allocated amounts of time in free-play via discovery, exploration and imagination. By the time they are five years old, they should be bursting with desire to continue learning because they are curious to explore the endless possibilities.

"THERE'S NEVER TIME TO DO ANYTHING RIGHT THE FIRST TIME, BUT THERE'S ALWAYS TIME TO DO IT AGAIN" – ONE OF THE FAMED *MURPHY'S LAWS*

Is it so much to ask that we get children started on the right track for happy human development, or must we insist on tragically putting ourselves through double and triple the work in adulthood to get rid of issues that should have never been there in the first place? It sounds cruel, but definitely worth asking. Getting a proper head-start prepares us to live by our intended talents and the fulfillment we can derive from them. We are going to spend at least some of our mental lives contemplating the purpose of our existence despite status quo concepts about how things are supposed to be. The question is, do we want to spend a major part of our lives exploring what's broken inside of us before we even reach the starting line of purposeful fulfillment? – Or, would we rather spend our lives exploring our endless opportunities for knowledge, and the experience of fulfillment from our abilities and the contributions we can make from them?

Language empowers us with words and expressions to act upon what we feel, think, learn, understand, and experience. A "Positive-Development-Dialect" comprised of phrases and expressions that are filled with what we **can** <u>do</u>, <u>think</u>, and <u>feel</u> defines what we intend to fulfill, rather than focus on what is missing or what seems impossible.

By learning and utilizing a dialect of positive terminology, we can re-construct the cognitive process of our intended potentials and collaborate a legacy of ability for one another and the generations that follow.

CONSTRUCTIVE CRITICISM VS. DESTRUCTIVE CRITICISM

The general philosophy about positivity would be incomplete without reviewing the concept of criticism. If ever a term was used loosely or frighteningly inverted, it is that paradoxically misguided and sometimes thoughtless offering of solicited or unsolicited "constructive criticism". It is daring to say, but constructive criticism may be so rare, it could very well be listed under the same definition as deception in the dictionary.

However *well-intended*, few people realize that in the midst of counseling mutually mis-guided souls, they are offering little or zero knowledge about making positive changes, and the advice is usually packaged in *de*-structive criticism, or vague and useless advice. Even when the rare occasion of constructive criticism is offered, most of us have become defensively clouded and unable to tell the difference because we are still reverberating from the effects of shame that accompanied bouts of judgmental criticism we received as children. <u>Con</u> from Latin, means <u>with</u>, *con*-structive criticism means criticism with structure; creative options, something someone can build upon. The truth is, if we were actually acclimated and well-versed in the literal positive semantics of constructive criticism, if it were a regular part of our communication skills, and generous helpings of it were available, we would eat it up. It would be, it could be, a regularly welcome and natural element of our interaction skills.

In young children's development, one of the most deceptive practices of destructive criticism is dispensed in the form of labeling. It may masquerade as a cute way of tolerating undesirable attributes that are actually indicative of potential abilities, but it is a direct and unkind method of judgment that can produce a prophesy of self admonition. If you are engaging in this practice, cease it immediately, or replace it with a term or endearment that reflects one of your Child's better characteristics. In addition to that, if you are talking about your children in their presence, consider how you'd feel if someone did the same to you.

WHAT IS DISCIPLINE - REALLY!

Is discipline really about restricting ourselves, or refraining from unconstructive and undesirable pursuits? Or is it about working ourselves to the bone in spite of the need to stop for food and water? Perhaps! However, *discipline,* when reserved and applied to a field of talent, referred to as a "discipline", would defy the need to waste it only on formidable behavior because it is being used exhaustively and otherwise - in positive constructive pursuit of our ever refining talents and potentials.

Positive vocabulary should be the basis for all teaching techniques in Early Childhood Education. It could be readily integrated into all forms of teaching, and training in sequential levels of development and in all disciplines.

Because Positive Vocabulary and Terminology constitute a Dialect, it is best learned the same way any language is learned and spoken well – early, when there is little comprehensive struggle or effort to absorb it. The younger children are when you begin speaking in Positivity, the easier it will be to mutually communicate in that language.

By utilizing the conversion or translation of Positivity, (especially before the age of seven), the easier it will be to avoid reverting back to the mother tongue of negative language semantics that was the formerly accepted dialect for guidance. Perhaps together with your children and even your friends, you will enjoy the process of learning a new language that identifies and expresses all the indications of advantages and possibilities.

PART TWO

X

FACT AND FICTION

"An Interview"

I N THE ATTEMPT TO present some of the additional processes, moods and requisites of preschool stage development that would seem technically cumbersome in a prose format, this section presents a *hypothetical* *interview* with *fictionalized* characters. It is designed to give you an insider's view, about the wonder, fascination, curiosity, and confusion in the life of a preschooler. Furthermore, it serves as a reminder about some of the expectations and ideas we have either forgotten or dismissed regarding children's rights and capabilities.

THE CHARACTERS

Lance and *Miekala* are the interviewers, who propose interrogative and objective questions that support conventional views about early development.

Lance leans toward the school of thought that children should follow all requests and directions from parents and caretakers without question or challenge.

Miekala, on the other hand lacks any strict viewpoints about raising children, but looks forward to hearing the voice behind the happy and convivial disposition of children.

The principle character and sole interviewee is a 4-year old girl named Eve, who wishes to express her view-point about what it feels like to be a Child and what constitutes the impulses of preschool children. Eve's intention is to connect you with the psyche of children, and the memory of being a Child, as we all once were.

Any 4-year old, would seem oddly pretentious if she could contemplate, let alone explain, what it means to be in the preschool stage of development. Moreover, it would be impossible for her to make any hypothetical conclusions about what she experiences or the conceptions and comparisons she believes adults maintain about Early Childhood education. However, for this interview's sake, she will assume the intellect of an adult while she attempts to reconnect you with the experiences of growing up in a big complicated world.

Eve is altruistic, as is characteristic of young children, but she, like any Child, faces the challenges of growing up. Eve presents her ideas with literal and abstract analogies in an attempt to dispel some misconceived notions about the energetic and sometimes unpredictable antics of children's behavior. Eve believes that we each possess an intuitive aptitude for understanding and accepting truthful premises, and she is prepared to express herself straightforwardly in accordance with that understanding.

In her wisdom we might join her in challenging the fears that cloak our hearts true desires and the vulnerabilities we submit to pain and rejection instead of potential.

In an effort to display whatever virtues she feels may further improve the relationships and communication between adults and children, she forthwith apologizes for any offensiveness or discomfort she may imbue during the course of this interview.

She speaks on behalf of preschool children everywhere, regardless of culture, race, gender, religion, nationality, or the era of history they've lived in.

"The Interview"

Miekala (M): Eve, Thank you for coming her today. To begin, what would you like to tell us about?

Eve (E): I guess I'm here to tell you about what children want and I'd like to connect a few dots here and there about our process of development.

Lance (L): What makes you think that we can really learn <u>anything</u> from a four-year-old? There are plenty of sources available from experts for folks who want to understand parenting techniques.

E: Well before we get started, you must keep in mind **that this is about what it feels like to be a Child**. How could <u>I</u> tell <u>you</u> what it's like to be a parent when I've never been one?! Only a parent can tell you what it's like to be a parent. It would be a divergence of my purpose here if I were proposing that I could tell you about parenting. I'm here to do my best to tell you about us, and help folks remember what it's like to be a Child. Why do adults insist that when you mention *Child* development, that it is all about how the *parents* feel?

L: That's a good point, I never actually thought of it that way.

E: It's simply like this; since it is parents' decision to bring children into the world, they feel that the whole process has to do with their feelings in the matter of children's development. By the time people are parents they have usually outgrown their Child-like mind, the one they left behind when they were told it was time to grow up.

This interview is an occasion to recapture the memories, feelings and motives of what it was like when you were a kid yourself.

L: I remember what I thought when I was a Child, I have a very good memory.

E: Ah, yes, but do you remember *how* you thought? What made you think the way you did, why others actions and reactions affected you the way they did - in a certain manner?

L: I'd have to be honest and say that I would be unable to make that kind of assessment.

E: Well, thank you for being honest. I'd like to take you back to your Childhood Lance, did you ever have a dog?

L: I always wished for one, but never had one. What does that have to do with raising children?

E: How about you Miekala?

M: Yes, I had a dog.

E: Great, let's start with this, how do you train a dog?

M: Well! – we hope.

E: That is the expectation. But if I told you that it was sufficient for a trainer to just let a dog loose in a training pen, without any leading or directions and then anticipate that the dog would do everything the trainer had in mind, what would you think about that?

L: That's ridiculous.

E: Precisely. A good trainer knows that the dog must be put on a tight leash and led through the motions of expected behavior, and incidentally, expert trainers always reward dogs in training for fulfilling the tasks and directions they are led through. The trainer never wastes any time reprimanding the dog.

L: Are you comparing dogs to kids?

E: Hardly. But what I'm saying is that if the dog gets to have that much specific training and rewards, children should be as worthy of that kind of discipline and attention too. Why should we get anything less?

M: That's a really good point.

E: Thank you. The point is that the dog trainer is never deceived by the idea that the dog will do everything correctly without specific directions. Imagine the trainer just standing by with his arms crossed, waiting for the creature to be a good little doggy without any help or directions. Then when the pup does something wrong, the trainer would chase him down, grab his paw and slap it announcing what a bad doggy he is.

L: That sounds like my Childhood. I see your point. So you are saying that children should be put on a tight leash too?

E: Well, I'd like to forfeit the leash part, but symbolically speaking, yes! We are begging for the kind of guidance and security that gives us direction to explore freely and naturally. You know how adults crave peace and solitude from time to time? Well, it's that kind of feeling.

L: I understand the analogy, and I dare say you are bringing a few more things to mind about my own Childhood that I'd forgotten.

E: Good, I want you to understand how feelings from early Childhood span across our lifetimes. The Child you thought was totally grown up is still looking for guidance and security. In moments of peace and solitude, you're either fostering the good guidance you've received and wondering what you can do next in your life, or finding a way to heal the security and encouragement that was missed.

Regardless of social, economic, cultural, historical or political conditions and demands, the requisites for our development are the same, and have always been so.

M: So, could you give us some more details, what else is specifically necessary for this stage of growth?

E: Gladly, the last thing I want to be is *vague*, that has been an all too consuming burden for children, that is one of my major topics. Specifics are underestimated and they're so much more prescriptive to what we need. We are a conglomerate of complexities just as you are, with the difference of course that we are still emerging, growing and understanding the world around us.

Our basic compositions resemble grown people, we encapsulate emotions, a mind, a willful nature and our souls are like open books, each of our personal stories have yet to be written. We possess a capacity to become competent and accomplish things provided we are nurtured. We need the nutrients of love, affection, understanding, discipline, acceptance, toughness, compassion, and encouraging support to develop our talents and abilities, and become competent individuals.

L: That sounds ideal, and it would be really ideal if everybody received all that.

E: I agree, and I know there are plenty of children in the world who are getting a lot less than that, but truth be told, that is what it really takes to raise us. We all need to live a productive life and feel fulfilled. Some of our best opportunities in life happen when we have developed our Special talents and potentials.

M: Could you please tell us your take on developing potentials and talents then?

E: Sure. These are the things that identify who each and every one of us are, they are our personal signatures of distinct uniqueness. But most importantly, when dispensed with those nutrients they are a major venue for happiness and fulfillment. Each of us has a creative talent or ability inside us longing to be recognized, refined and revealed to others with whom we interact. We are lucky to be living in a time where we *can* pursue any way of life, including finding personal fulfillment through our talents.

I believe that many people suffer because of their lost dreams or worse, never having discovered them. We are at a threshold where our emotional and spiritual needs make us seriously question the purpose of physical survival. But the cat is out of the bag, we now know that all people deserve and are entitled to equal and total survival and fulfillment of all our senses and desires.

L: So, I guess you know that I would ask you how we could contemplate pursuing total survival when there are so many people struggling with basic physical survival?

E: Obviously, there is quite an imbalance. I will answer your question this way. We, humans are creatures of duality, like every part of nature. When babies are first born, they need to be held and touched and they need to suckle and eat, you can easily find plenty of evidence to support the importance of all those needs. That is Nature's blueprint of the way life is, we all start out needing help as babies, so helping others in need would naturally seem like part of the greater development scheme. But real help means that dual developments have to be addressed simultaneously for all people, if human beings are to experience real survival and true fulfillment. There are a lot of changes that must be made in human development.

L: Do you mean religion or politics?

E: Neither. We already discussed the nutrients for development and fulfillment. How many adults that you know can honestly say, they'd rather live without love, fulfillment, compassion and happiness? Everybody wants them, because everybody needs them. They constitute the purpose of living, so we need to learn them as children.

Why else would we need those elements except to be real whole adults? Fundamentally, we inherit these nutrients, they are *given* to us, that's the set-up of human kind. We socialize as families because it is our natural inclination to do so, and we receive our first experiences of human development from our families.

But trust me on this – we are all interconnected in such a way that there can only be so much of a gap between the hungriest person and the most enlightened person. Human consciousness depends on the advancement of all people - all individuals. It's a civilization process. Think of it this way. You know how to count, you can understand numbers with endless digits. But before the discovery of zero, a person who could count to 9 was only ever so slightly smarter - mathematically - than the person who was unable to count at all. During those times, folks were limited to a certain knowledge or intelligence which tied their consciousness together. So even the most fulfilled person is bound by the merit and consciousness of the times and conditions we live in, and everyone's plight and destiny is going to be effected by that.

It's a natural phenomenon, because all elements of the world, whether they are 3-dimensional or 4 or 5 or 12-dimensional, are interconnected and tied together. There are plenty of folks who will dispute or deny that, but they're fooling themselves. Take away the people they love and the things they love to do, and you will see the 5th dimension crumble inside of that 3-D person.

L: I appreciate that. So, for the purpose of development, can you clarify these obligations of physical and fulfillment survival or whatever these tendencies are that we all have?

E: First, obviously, there are children's physical needs ~ Providing food, water, shelter, and then teaching children how to function in the world by learning to provide for themselves independently when they eventually become adults.

L: And the other...?

E: Let's put it this way. Some people are just disciplinarians in their children's lives and others are just talent scouts. Still, others offer plenty of affection and love but may fall short of implementing structure, and naturally there are some who manage to integrate all these elements.

Many people focus on building self-esteem as though it is a goal in itself for contentment, achievement or fulfillment. The nutrients of care, compassion, guidance and nurturing have to have a portal. Is it enough to just look at food if you're hungry? You have to put it in its necessary portal. It has to go in your mouth, you have to eat it. Even love itself has to have a trajectory or venue for dispensing. It may seem or feel like a "pie in the sky" dream. But love itself is formless and boundless, and our creative natures call us to rapture its energy into constructive rapport. That's just a fancy way of saying that love has to have a portal too. It needs definition.

You know how even as adults, you are attracted to certain people because they match your own inclinations and terms of conscientious love and common interests. That is the pathway or portal of your interactive relationship. For children too, there are portals for love and interaction, and you can consider our individual talents to be one of those main portals. Children like to feel attractive too. We feel pride and independence when we can do tasks competently or by ourselves. In terms of loving unconditionally, talents and abilities are very clear indications of who we are. When you recognize, accept and guide our personal abilities, we feel loved.

If you want to love and accept us for who we are, then you have to take each of our particular abilities into account. Spoiling has nothing to do with loving too much. Spoiling is allowing children to decide their own impulsive needs and desires without fostering their practical capabilities or individual talents. That's what guidance is. It's about putting our boundless energy, needs and desires into constructive activities that appeal to our capabilities. It's about allowing us to do tasks that we can actually do by ourselves.

If you alter or withhold love according to who you want us to be or make us feel guilty or wrong about our uniqueness, then that's what classifies conditional love for us, the children.

Self-esteem is really a by-product of constructive, active and interactive love. If you are looking to build self-esteem as an attribute in itself, that would be like trying to toss coal into the wind and expecting it to land in a specifically intriguing formation, or that the coal would instantly, magically become diamonds.

If you're feeling confused or wonder how much of a Child's talents you've been able to nail down, genuine encouragement will do the trick too. If children are positively guided without closed-and-shut, uncreative options, at least they'll be in a position to discover their own capabilities later on, if they want to.

M: I'm glad to hear that, it is a refreshing understanding of the concept of self-esteem. So how do we recognize these talents or individual abilities, what do we look out for?

E: I'll admit that it feels as though you have to pluck it out of obscurity. But a little investigative work can put it in the mainstream for you. Every important job requires a little paperwork. This is what you have to do: You have to start your own journal. Commit to dedicating two "15-minute" sessions a week to watching us play and write down what you observe. But there's a little catch.

L: I knew there had to be a catch.

E: You'll survive it, trust me.

L: That's very funny.

E: I was trying to be serious. Joking is something I still have a hard time understanding, it involves too many abstract ideas. You are certainly welcome to introduce us to the idea, but funny to us is something we absorb through our physical senses like watching a clown or being tickled, and stay away from scary things please. Reality, fantasy and imagination are all the same to us, that's why we get upset and cry from nightmares, or from someone telling us about a frightening proposition.

So, let's get started. First, be sure you are observing a different activity each time - playing inside, playing outside, playing alone or with friends, and watch the things we gravitate toward. Sometimes you'll have to prepare an activity. Oh, and here's the real catch, you have to pretend you are a video-recorder, you have to describe exactly what you see without any personal opinions or judgments.

One more thing, you have to give us some opportunities to play with messy or dirty things. Just before each new observation, take a minute to read your last observation. After a couple of months, you will see certain patterns of movement, inclinations or impulses. The last thing is, you have to refrain from interfering *unless* there's a safety issue that comes up.

M: That's it - then what?

E: Well, for one thing, you'll probably notice rather quickly what things we like and what sort of things we dislike, that's one pretty concrete clue. You have to experience it for yourself, everyone's revelation is going to be different, you come back and tell me about it, okay?

M: All right. What's the point of doing some messy play, you know there's a lot of people who dislike messes, do the kids clean up the mess?

E: Thanks for asking. Things in the natural world are usually kind of messy, and they are our basis for understanding science. If you know anyone who feels they lack an understanding of physical science, look into their Childhood and it's probably very likely they had few opportunities to play with the physical, natural world. The name of the game in our development is diversification, do you think we really know the difference between math or science or reading books or cleaning? They're all part of the same conglomerated-interconnected subject to us. Restricting us from playing with parts of the natural world is only going to restrict our connection to it and our understanding of it. If you treat cleaning with the same attitude that you treat story-time, what do you think that'll be like? Sing a song, get creative, take a picture and send it to Grandma.

Hey, messes are just as "wonderful" as a building block structure we put together, cleaning it up is just as exciting as making snow-angels, if you act like it is. The only reason we try to escape it, is usually because adults have attached this dreary, gloomy mood to the whole process, either when you do it or ask us to do it. We've got one mission – to have fun. Make cleaning fun and we'll be more than happy to do it.

L: You make it sound so simple, you really are idealistic.

E: Hey, I'm 4-years old.

L: Okay, but what if you do try to escape your responsibility to clean up, should you be reprimanded?

E: Everybody's an expert at reprimands and punishments, and looking for the disadvantages in situations. Do you really believe children are poorly disciplined because they are insufficiently reprimanded?

L: Well, I have to say that has been my viewpoint about poorly disciplined kids.

E: Thanks for being honest again. Lance. But the real matter is that in most cases, we are poorly behaved because we are insufficiently rewarded for our efforts. When we get properly rewarded or given praise for things we are supposed to do, then that's *direction*, that's creating a desire in us to do things you want us to do, things we're supposed to do. We're always going to be doing something, and we're always going to be looking for attention and recognition, so give us a break here.

L: Once again, I'll accept that, but it's going to take a little time to process these new ideas.

E: Tell me about it, life's like that everyday for us. Sometimes people think you tell us something once and we got it.

M: We get that too, Eve.

L: Well, why should you get rewarded for things you're supposed to do. Maybe you'll grow up thinking you are always going to get rewarded for things you are supposed to do, or run into the habit of skipping your responsibilities unless you are sure you'll get something in return.

E: Oh yeah, I've heard about this issue, good thing you mentioned it. I think adults forget that we "think" in our feelings. Adults do too Lance, but they probably think more about how they feel, whereas we mostly just feel. The point is we all learn to feel before we learn to think about any and every idea. As kids we have very little intellectual experience, we've had to determine things by our feelings. So understanding and accepting the mental idea about the way something is supposed to be done is difficult because the intellectual world is really fuzzy wuzzy and confusing, but the emotional world is as real and concrete as our imaginations. We tend to feel by imagining it and vice versa. That really means that ideas go into our brains through our feelings. If you should need a definition of "supposed to", now you know how it's supposed to work for us.

We are in a stage of development where habits are easily acquired or broken. If you want desirable behavior to become a habit, you have to create a theme, a setting or atmosphere for it, once the feeling behind the task has gelled then it constitutes an idea and you can move onto other habits and creative themes to support them. Whenever an idea or task is re-presented, you can be sure that the feelings it was originally presented with are going to be there in our minds and hearts. That's why the feelings determine whether we are going to rise to the occasion of a task or run away. Rewards are just tools and tactics you use to create those feelings that are deposited in your bank of emotional intelligence. Feelings connected with certain tasks, responsibilities or situations then become the motivating or de-motivating factor for re-use. But I think your real concern would be if it would influence the way we think in the future.

L: Exactly.

E: Well you may hear us dabbling about the future, such as what we want to be when we grow up. It's impossible for us to project how we'll think in the future. We'd have to be able to theorize intellectually into the future about how experiences will influence us. In other words we'd have to know now about the knowledge we'd have in the future. We can only do what we're capable of now. Think about it, that expectation is based on a fear that we'd be unable to break certain habits, that's a justified concern. There's a developmental stage happening here.

Hopefully, by the time we are able to hypothesize, we'll be doing it with a more mature and sophisticated mind, instead of the one we have now. Do you make decisions now based on what you felt when you were four years old?

L: I doubt that I do, but I think I know one or two people who seem to.

E: That's frightening.

L: Tell me about it! You mentioned something like internal structure before, can you tell us a little about that?

E: You bet. Well as you know, my main concern is about receiving specific positive directions. Think about the "Big Bang Theory." The beginning of the universe was all this scattered energy and matter, then some force of logic pulled it all together and poof, you have galaxies everywhere. Yeah, I know, some people think it just happened by chance. You can go ahead and try that with us too. Just take a chance and leave all your logical intentions aside and see what happens to us. All energy, big and small needs some purpose and direction.

M: That's very interesting, it sounds like a theory to me, but what about this internal structure Lance asked about?

E: Sorry, I can get a little carried away sometimes. I was saying that we are like the big-bang theory, except we're just little mini-bang-theories and we have all this energy that's really scattered all over sometimes, well, a lot of the time. Let's create a scenario here. Suppose you are a Mom or Dad at home, working from home and taking care of the kids. You're running a business, and doing the shopping and cooking and cleaning and answering the phone, doing the laundry, running errands, paying the bills and juggling us in between.

M: I'm exhausted just hearing about it, I know people in situations like that, and they have very little time for their kids.

E: That's one challenge, and we talked about survival issues earlier.

People have to make a living, I understand that, I think. But this is what I would like to help you understand. These parents are busy, really busy. They have half the energy that we have and they are getting twice as many things done. Kids like to imitate their parents, and if you are so busy and we have double the energy you have, what on earth do you think we should be doing?

M: Playing, of course.

E: Yes, and do you think these parents are planning their work day?

M: Naturally, you have to plan your working day.

E: And it is a Kid's *job* to play, so our work day has to be planned too. You might remedy the chaos by creating consequences and requesting apologies for disturbing behavior, but all of those effects are happening because the internal structure, the children's workday was forlorn to start with.

It's fine to fix things that are broken, but it's better if they are never broken in the first place. You just have to be a fly on the wall, look and listen. Do, done, doing! These are the operative words of the parents day – and can you guess what they are saying to their kids all day long???

L: *"Don't do this and don't do that, and you can't do that...and you're not doing...* Let me guess what else is happening– they're mostly getting attention for doing things the parents disapprove of, and the parent is too busy to give them more attention for doing the right things.

E: Lance, you've been paying attention.

L: You see, old dogs can learn new tricks.

E: We're designed to do, just like you and with twice as much energy as adults, we should have a plan. I really do believe that parents can pull this off, they can make quality and quantity time for their kids. We're at your mercy, and if we're presented with choices and direction for playing then our day can be as organized and constructive as parents' working day. The lack of structure, planning or supervision means we can get into anything. When that happens, we can get our hands on things that are off-limits and that may be interpreted or judged as either bad behavior or a deliberate attempt to be uncooperative.

M: But we learned earlier that kids are naturally good, so what would make them play or act uncooperatively?

E: Everything in the world is a virtual magnet to our senses, we're curious and we want to explore. We're always aware of our parents' absence or presence, but with them or without them, we crave direction, need approval and need attention. Unconsciously, we're driven to do the kinds of things that will get us those needs. We're driven a lot by imagination and we can keep going until, or unless someone intervenes with some sensible direction. I know you've witnessed some Child pulling a few fast ones, even while someone is watching. I'm telling you, that Child is screaming for guidance. That kid is plain old scared and that's the only way to let somebody know. It might be very well masked in defiance, but let me tell you what that kid is feeling like.

L: I'd definitely be interested in knowing that.

E: Pretend tomorrow you got into your car, and hit the road, and suddenly all traffic signs and stop lights have been removed, traffic laws have been abolished. So, you're driving down the highway and all the dotted lines have been removed, the lanes are gone, and everyone is driving anyway they want. All road order has ceased to exist, how does that feel? Who gets to decide what the rules are, or does everybody just follow their own rules?

L: That is really scary, and needless to say it would be very dangerous confusing and disorderly.

E: And that is what it feels like for a Child who is constantly getting reprimanded, given negative direction most of the time, and very little direction or options about what they *can* do, or what's permissible, so they have to just test every option. That's their only way of saying, well, can I do this, or I want to do that, or what can I do?

M: You've given us a lot to think about, I'm unsure what to ask you about now. Lance, do you have anything on your mind to ask Eve?

L: Well, I hear parents debating about things such as how much Television kids should watch, or how much sugar they should eat, or if they should be allowed to eat it at all.

E: I guess I'm going to have to use the word diversification again. We have more than just one sense. So we need to do all kinds of things. Different experiences record different types of information in the brain. But too much or too little of any activity is just rough on the senses. Lance, you asked me about sugar - right?

M: Yes, he asked you - big controversy, this sugar thing.

E: Balancing and modifying are the last things on our minds, we'll leave that up to parents.

I'll give you some food for thought. Even our tongue has its own little diversification theme going on. Obviously, we're capable of tasting and enjoying flavors of all kinds. Nature is designed quite magnificently and correlates with many of the needs we all require. Our bodies have indicators for bodily functions. Your body tells you when to go to the bathroom or when to go to sleep, right? If you have an infection or are sick, you either come down with a fever or feel really strange and uncomfortable. So my answer to your question is this: Nature provides a variety of different resources and foods that take care of different needs for health and growth. Granted there are many people who are unable to consume certain things.

L: So you're saying that kids should eat sugar.

E: I'm saying that if we are burning twice as much energy as adults, and our bones and muscles are growing, then whatever protein we consume needs to be used for that. If we use protein for energy, what will we use for growth? Who would dare to tell a pregnant woman to deny her cravings? So why do you think kids crave sugar? Parents and caretakers should modify and diversify children's food intake, because children can get a little carried away with their cravings. I know sugar has received an unfavorable report. I know it's been overused, but is that sugar's fault? Totally eliminating it is only going to cause other problems.

Children crave sugar for a reason, and nature provides it. I think indications such as those should be regarded in the whole context of our interconnected world. There are resources everywhere that correlate with all of our needs. As things go, rather than look at how we've mishandled resources, we usually just blame the resource, how corrupt is that?! The body *is* originally designed to handle at least traces of sugary intake. If we were never meant to have sugar, then why do we have enzymes that digest it? There many folks whose bodies have trouble with the whole sugar challenge that can tell you what a nightmare it is to manage this function and digesting sugar *is* a necessary function. If we totally lacked the need for any kinds of broken down sugar substances, then all bodily functions would never miss them.

M: Yes, and I think we all know someone in that situation.

L: I still think that some people would really debate this whole sugar issue.

E: Well maybe adult bodies could do without it, but with the energy that children burn, I believe that sugar can come in quite handy. But my real claim here is to point out the idea of <u>variety</u> - it's as important to our bodies as it is to our learning skills.

L: Do you have a favorite food?

E: I really like sweets myself, especially chocolate, it's kind of spicy and tasty sweet at the same time, but I'm unsure about saying that there's one particular savory, spicy food out there that's my favorite. I'm sort of still discovering that. Every time I go to the supermarket with my mom, it's like a confusing adventure because I'm relying on pictures and labels to tell me a story and of course I'm constantly ripping things off the shelves to ask my mom their contents.

M: - And you're begging her to buy it for you?

E: Sometimes, but while we're on this subject, I do have a little pet peeve and I really want to pick a bone with this issue.

L: You already have a pet peeve?

E: I guess.

M: Okay, tell us about it.

E: Well, there's this little thing that adults do sometimes, actually a lot, and you know how people always say that it's the little things that matter in life?

L: Is this going to hurt?

E: Maybe. Let me give it to you straight up. It's more liberating than you think, but I'm going to petition you to take it seriously.

We need to explore making connections and in this case we need some guidance about placing things back where they belong with the use of our own hands, especially in that all too familiar scene at the supermarket or toy store. It's tempting for an adult to just take it away and put it back. It seems like the obvious thing to do and of course, all good intentions are behind it.

I think the best way to explain it is to say that if we can depart from the dearly desired object with our own hands, even if our will is hesitating, it gives us a sense of closure. I know life seems too busy to take the time to implement that little habit. It's frustrating for parents to watch children hesitate. A parent may wonder if the Child is challenging their authority and perhaps determine that hesitation as an act of misbehavior or defiance.

Most of the time, we may feel that there is still a chance to convince the parent about purchasing something. A Child may still be processing the direction, or even wonders if the parent really means what they are saying. Most of this can be avoided if we're briefed before entering the supermarket and told exactly what's going to be purchased on a previously-written list. Make a game out of it, delegate responsibilities, let us help. Silly little things like that mean a lot to us if we can do them with our own hands and you can help us keep our hands distracted. Aside from all that, we like feeling as though we are capable of doing important and necessary tasks.

It may seem like an impossible mission at first, but if it's done over and over again, it'll stick. You've got to keep in mind that if our capabilities are being confided in, then we feel welcome to cooperate. At any rate, these techniques are designed to help you and your kids function in a more serene and peaceful atmosphere. It's really a lot less trouble than it seems. The other thing to keep in mind is that unlike adults who need at least a month to get rid of, or change a habit, it really only takes about two weeks for us, so give us another break here.

L: That sounds fair.

E: Yeah, well I wish everything was fair.

M: What do you mean?

E: Well, fair is very subjective to everyone, especially to children. Fairness works in conjunction with an ability to reason. Although our priority is to play and have fun, this skill for reasoning can make fairness feel very confusing.

Unfortunately, when we're being guided, we are sometimes spoken to with the assumption that our skills of thinking reasonably are intact. All people contain some instinctive understanding about right and wrong. Since fair to us has to do with the reality of our own situations then fair can have some pretty strange definitions from where we stand.

L: So Eve, where do you stand on how to handle right and wrong?

E: If we follow the system for real positive development, focusing on "right" and "good" is going to be better guidance then saying what's all "wrong" with something or someone. Our heads need to be filled with good, right and able information. If you were studying for a test, would you bother studying all the wrong answers? Never! You'd study all the right answers. It's amazing how much negative guidance you can hear all around you if you just stop and listen. You'll hear folks saying how things can go wrong, or find them preparing for the worst. Sometimes it can be wise advice, but overall, everyone desires favorable outcomes. Just sit down in a public place sometime and make the observation for yourself, and the funny part of it is that most people have really good intentions in mind. Often, when it comes to giving advice, common words of wisdom are patronizing and vague, even for adults. But it's a regular practice to just accept it without question, and those who do question it are rebutted for being unappreciative of good counsel.

M: Can you give us an example?

E: Sure, "Be careful".

L: That's good advice.

E: For what?

L: For whatever.

E: Excuse me for playing the cynic here, but "be careful" in one situation would be useless advice in another. It might as well be used as a farewell salutation. "Be careful" is a worthy phrase, but it needs to be further classified into something specific, especially for us young inexperienced folk. We need to hear relative phrases such as 'hold that with two hands' 'go slowly' 'keep your fingers away from the closing door'! Stuff like that, you know. It's just really embarrassing to hear someone say "I told you so" after something happens, when all they said was "be careful."

M: Lance, I think I'd have to agree with that, what do you think?

L: Well, yes it's embarrassing for us adults to hear "I told you so" too.

E: And that's exactly the sort of thing I'm talking about. Hey, I like a good "pop-term" as much as the next gal, but when good meaning - especially vague - advice turns into a pop-term, it kind of lets people off the hook of actually offering smart advice when and where it may be needed. It's the same with so many other things we hear and say. I think there are a lot of important terms that lose their allure and proficiency to the ridiculous or to vagueness, and if you challenge someone on it, just try it, you'll see for yourself that most folks will have trouble spelling it out for you. If they do, I'll bet you most of it will be described with negations, or they'll feel mistrusted by your questioning them - that's my bet, are you up for it?

L: I think you're getting carried away again.

E: Yeah, I am, it's a little overboard, and exaggerated, but I want to stretch the idea about generic counsel and virtually unconscious, recycled words of warning, predestined consequences, and ultimatums that are expressed in the name of good conscience by vaguely familiar terms.

L: I think that's a bit radical.

M: I think so too, are you sure positivity has gotten the best of you?

E: Yeah, maybe, but I just wanted to stress the importance of being specific. Sometimes I think you have to explore outside of the lines.

M: Explore what?

E: What you believe and say and think.

L: Where are you going with this?

E: At some point it's always a good idea to dissect or even invalidate what you hear, accept or believe. Think of it this way; if someone else tried to invalidate what you believe, how could you defend and honor what you think or believe if you've never explored it enough to understand it on your own? We can become quite accustomed to accepting certain things without question, but you've got to be able to turn your own beliefs and ideas inside out yourself if you want to call them your own. You've got to do a little exploration and find out what it's made of, sort of like having discovered it on your own. If you fall for everything others tell you, how can you really stand up for it? People should never stop exploring just because they've grown out of childhood. Adults spend more time thinking and less time playing, so this is a way of keeping exploration alive. I know some people would just call that faith, but if faith was a prelude for everything that everyone told you or an excuse for lacking the inclination to educate yourself, then what would be the use of having critical thinking skills anyway?

But where am I going with this, you might ask? We're in the position to qualify ideas, but ideas should never qualify us. It's the same for morals or advice or anything like that.

M: You're saying that even though morals and advice are good, people should qualify it before they take it on for themselves.

L: Yes, I would have to agree with that because many folks take others advice without thinking too much about it.

E: This is one of those instances where I believe you can trace a direct line between how you process feelings as an adult and how you learned to process them as a child. If we're judged instead of guided, we have to give up our own feelings. It's a vicious cycle of denial and mixed emotional ownership. When it's your turn to give advice, you've learned you have to give your feelings with it - of course you're going to feel rejected if your advice is rejected. If you were really owning your own feelings would you give them away that easily? You would just give advice and let others own their own feelings with it.

M: That is considerably major, who would've thought about it like that. But parents have a right to react to behaviors that are offensive.

L: Yeah, Eve maybe it's just your idealism talking again, and this is really one of those situations that people will never find a way to get around.

E: Okay, so this is where I tell you about the serious task of asking questions.

M: Who's asking the questions?

E: It works both ways.

L: You mean that we should ask you questions to things we want to know more about?

E: What I have in mind has nothing to do with giving adults advice or anything like that. When we're young, we possess a natural gift for asking questions, because we are natural explorers. But as people get older they seem to lose the knack for asking questions, they've been fed so many demands and expected to just have "faith", or to accept things without question. When older folks stop asking questions, they stop asking us questions too. By the way, asking yourself questions is one way to practice your own critical thinking skills, and it works well for qualifying or invalidating ideas that others divulge or insist that you adopt for yourself. You really have to start trusting your own instincts.

New or multi-directional tasks can be a bit confusing. If we're upset, sick or sad we may be misunderstanding or mis-processing directions. Parents may feel that what they say "just goes in one ear and out the other." The point is that our communication skills are still developing and it's easy for us to feel excluded from a conversation.

Remember, we need learning to include diversification of functions and our brains work better if we are in a position to use more than one sense to process information. So if you just <u>tell</u> us a command or direction, we only get to use our ears, but if you reiterate a direction with a question, then we get to use our verbal skills and our ears and we have to listen to the direction twice. The best part of it is that when we hear ourselves say the direction it touches our intuitive skills. It's because we learn through our senses, so the more senses we use, the easier it is to learn something. It's a quaint little trick, also in the instances that parents are addressing a misdeed, it gives parents a chance to take a breath and think before bundling us with the acts of poor behavior.

We often feel a little pressed with our own independence, all by myself is a motto that's very close to our hearts. It helps to hear our own voice say or repeat a direction. It lends the illusion that we are telling ourselves what to do, and it's less likely that we would argue with ourselves, or go against our own word.

You'll get a song and dance here and there, but stick with it, it works like a charm if you use it consistently.

M: That sounds like a really smart piece of *advice.*

E: Well try it out for yourself sometime and I promise you, you will faithfully believe the results for yourself.

L: Do you have a recommended or standard question that works?

E: Lance, you already know how I feel about generic and vague statements, so I'd feel the same way about generic questions. But there is a standard technique. It's always worth putting an alternative in your question, unless your question is to entice us to repeat directions that we must get started on immediately. You'll figure some of them out for yourself, but there are plenty of samples in the next section here to refer to.

L: Well how about if a Child is being ostentatious or silly and pretending that you are asking some other question altogether?

E: Consider it their exploration of Language Arts, you might want to go along with the game for a minute or two.

L: And then what?

E: And then go back to the original question.

L: Is that the only concrete advice you have?

E: We're people with creative dynamics, and who's supposed to know your children better than you do? You've got to work with that, have some fun with us, we're kids.

L: I guess I keep overlooking that factor.

E: Oh, and by the way, we love a warning with a little time element, so that we can make transitions - just another one of those little things that we'll save all of us some unnecessary frustration.

M: What's an ideal time warning? How much time do these transitions typically require.

E: Ten minutes works quite well, with a five-minute reminder in the middle of that ten minutes, and it helps us to develop a concept of time. Having a big clock in our play area will help us learn the purpose of telling time, but we need to have a traditional round clock with a face and hands on it. This way you can point out what 5 minute increments are, or show us when our time is up when one or both of the hands will reach certain spots. Another tip that adults may use is to put in writing something you want us to remember, put our name on it and make sure we see you writing it.

Sometimes kids want something that a parent promises and because we lack a concept of time, we'll just keep asking about it. Did you say 5 minutes from now or 5 days from now - think I know the difference? A big calendar comes in handy too, jot down special events and upcoming activities. Write us a note and give it to us for safe-keeping in our pocket or on our night table. We may have a year or two before learning to read and write, but if you've told us what you've written and read it to us, we'll remember it, trust me. We'll also feel important enough knowing that what we want or what we feel is worthy, it's just as much fun as being read a story.

L: I like that technique, Eve what other tips do you have?

E: Well, I have a few other points to mention before we bring this to a close, and I hope that I will have been able to assemble and tie together some very old notions and perhaps some new notions about the basic blueprint for our development.

By some of the requirements I've voiced so far, it may seem as though parents feelings are being totally ignored.

M: It may look like that to some folks.

E: Indeed, my heart goes out to them. Because we, the children, are really unaware of the sacrifices that parents make and the extra steps they go through to comfort and take care of us, but we are proud of them too, just because we love them.

L: So how would you like to conclude, what are a few of the other points you wanted to mention?

E: One of parents' main concerns is to see their Child learning social graces and growing up to be a caring individual. They may constantly worry that they will abhor themselves for having raised a selfish person. But anything done in such a push or rush just because you worry that some undesirable trait or habit will cement itself into our personality before we develop our own sense of decency - rest assured, everything is a process! And this process requires some really important steps that is you miss them, well then, the very thing you're trying to avoid could become a long drawn-out struggle. And it's worse for us because we have to deal with our own social development - ultimately.

M: What process are you specifically thinking about?

E: It's about this sharing thing. Some matters will make or break the difference between cooperation or frustrating disagreements. If you examine many of the age appropriate toys that preschoolers use, they are really designed for individual use. Sharing these toys, literally would mean cutting them in pieces.

I should just point out here that some things are never meant to be shared, but I will leave that to your imaginations to figure out.

For a 3 or 4 or 5 year old to give up one of these toys, even for a period of five minutes is a confusing proposition, especially when they are still figuring out time and the feelings and conditions of ownership. In other words, if parents force children to share or tell them they have to, because that is just the way things are supposed to be, or that they are being selfish, it's black and white here, that is totally wrong.

M: Why? Every parent throughout all the generations has been doing this.

E: Yes, I know. First, you are basically telling the Child, 'Oh, by the way, there are conditions to owning that toy I gave you, I never gave it to you unconditionally, it's subject to my commands and decisions'. It may sound a bit over dramatic, but in essence, that is what you are saying. You're saying that their feelings are invalid in these situations, and they have to relinquish their feelings and their possessions. There is nothing anywhere that says that children must share. But children should learn to share and there is a pattern and process to that development as there is any other.

So, I'll tell you what. If you want children to learn how to share from their own hearts and by their own accord, then lovingly encourage them to take turns. Use rewards, use a timer, there are all kinds of tricks. But if they are against the idea on a particular day or with a new item, then criticizing them is only going to backfire. Children need opportunities to learn the dynamics of ownership and how to be in control of their own things.

On the other hand, you may see a Child become the complete saint, because that may be the only time they receive encouragement and reinforcement from the parent, when they share on the parents terms. If a Child loses all sense of possession, what do you think that will equal?

M: What?

E: Well, Meikala you can only value something fully, if you own it fully, - true?

M: True.

E: So, if you want a Child to own the responsibility for taking care of those toys, then he has to feel as though he actually owns the toys. You have to own both. It's kind of unfair or unbalanced to own something and lack a sense of feeling of responsibility for it. By the same token, why should you be made to feel fully responsible for something that you lack a feeling of ownership for? A Child's feelings about their things should be respected as much as an adults feeling about their things. Forcing anybody to do something against their feelings is a poor lesson in respect and dignity.

L: Sounds heavy, but I see where that makes sense because I experienced a lot of that.

E: Indeed, it is and it's often awkward for parents to make the change, because they are so conditioned about what is socially good or acceptable behavior.

L: So you're saying we really need to get a proper start on these developments, right?

E: Yes, the seeds of our abilities can take many different turns depending on how they are nurtured, and what our natural dispositions, and influences are. There is always a prevalent argument about different individuals developing differently even when they have been exposed to the same circumstances. This premise has been used to prove or disprove as a generic formula for how to raise children. I know I mentioned this idea earlier. After all we've explored together here, I believe it's clearly acceptable that different talents need different disciplines. What's adventurous for one person is difficult for another person. As an old saying goes - "One man's junk is another man's treasure". Remember, poor behavior is just an aptitude or ability that has been given little constructive direction or unjustly judged and criticized. This is a very intricate matter that really needs to have a stick shaken at it.

M: You mean helping create happy, capable kids?

E: Yes, I want to convey what it means to speak to the abilities inside of a Child. We discussed the importance and value of asking questions and how it can help parents take a moment to look past the superficial effect of a behavior. You realize that taking offense to disrespectful behavior, or disrespectful communication would be very similar to taking offense to a Child simply because he has a fever. You understand that the Child and the fever are two different things, the Child has the fever. But you would never accuse the Child of *being* the fever, you simply want to take it away. Disrespectful behavior in very similar to a fever, something is brewing inside, and you want to take it away, that is why you want to separate children from whatever is *ailing* them, whether physical, emotional or otherwise. In both cases, it is up to the parent to take notice.

Fevers are, of course, a little more straightforward, and disrespect takes a little more exploration. It could be something they ingested emotionally two or three days ago. It can be very unnerving for parents, especially if they are unaccustomed to exploring emotions, all the while having to recall incidences in the child's day that come and go as quick as lightening. But asking questions will come in handy here, such as, 'Did something happen yesterday that you are still sad about'? - 'Are you still upset because we had to leave the party early'?... etc. Specific questions will do the same job as an aspirin for fever. The trick is to accept the answer without judgment or criticism and with plenty of compassion.

You've got to see through to the ability and point out positive options. Instead of telling a Child she is being lazy, a worthier presentation would be, 'Are you just thinking about the next thing you're going to do, or do you need help figuring something out'? – This is less patronizing and far more dignifying. So what if they want to do nothing? What's the worst that can happen? You might have a meaningful conversation with your own kid. What's that worth?

L: Makes me wish I was a Child now, so I can do it all over again. But I have a concern that's been on my mind for quite some time now.

E: Tell us. Lance.

L: I grew up in a community where so many children were denied the opportunities to be children, and I know others still who were neglected and abused. Several, have now become parents themselves, what do you see coming for these folks?

E: Anyone who has missed having a Childhood has to come to terms with that first. Many people have missed so much, and feel so relieved to be on their own that they proceed unaware of what they were entitled to.

If you review the primary information here, you will recollect that the requirements for all children's development is the same for everyone and always has been so all throughout history, for all children, of all backgrounds. For their sake and their children's sake, they are entitled to at least know what they deserved, and also if they should feel selfish or guilty for having wanted a happy Childhood, it's worth finding a way to explore and get rid of that guilt before they materialize their own sense of deprivation into their own children.

M: How does that work?

E: The path from pain, rejection and guilt is a long and dreary road, and whoever traversed it has it recorded in all of their senses and intelligence quotients. You know whatever road you came up on is the same road you have to travel back on in order to uncover what ails the heart and soul, and that is what makes change so painfully difficult. There are plenty of professionals who help people reverse and manage their tragedies and I'd like to see them putting their heads together so that all the diversified facets and cognitive processes can be addressed and mended. I know it sounds a bit utopian, but I'd like to see that happen.

M: So, have you covered all of what you intended to tell us?

E: I have one or two more points I'd like to challenge. Up until now, I've intended to explain something about the impulses, potentials, and natural inclinations that we have, but there are daily situations and interventions that parents have to utilize to maintain peaceful and happy conditions.

L: You mean practical everyday details.

E: Precisely. There are plenty of instances where we can become out of control or get carried away and measures must be implemented to balance an environment that everyone can feel safe and secure in.

M: Do you mean standard discipline?

E: If you like! Specifically, what should consequences be and what is the purpose and intention of implementing them.

L: Such as a time-out?

E: You've read my mind. I suppose we could combine a couple of these concerns. I feel that time-out has been overused and used in situations that are useless. For one, a time-out that is being given upon arrival at home for an incident that happened a half-hour ago fails to have the desired effect.

After everything I've explained, by now you might realize that a time-out would be a last resort and should only be used if it can be implemented at the time and place of a misdeed. Stop and ask yourself what your intention is, if it is your intention to punish, then – congratulations! Nothing else needs to be said about it.

My primary concern is that any method or measure of discipline that warrants a consequence should be relative to the circumstance. There has to be some kind of correlation. If you send your Child to her room because she spilled her milk, it's so far removed from addressing the issue, that you might as well send her to the moon for the rest of her life. If the milk has spilled for the one-hundredth time, because she always puts it in target range of her elbow movements, you may have to consider that you have hardly ever shown her exactly where the cup of milk should be placed - within arm's reach, and at an arm's distance. If that was the last drop of milk, she is already going to suffer a natural consequence – that's enough punishment.

Simply give her a sponge and apologize for forgetting to remind her that the cup should occupy a particular spot on her place-setting. On the other hand, if you have reminded her right then and there, in addition to countless other times, and she defiantly refuses, then you might send her to her room to think about it for two minutes before returning to the table to finish her meal.

But I promise you this. Show me someone who is telling this Child over and over and over again, and I'll show you someone who is using negative guidance and assuming this Child's inability to keep a cup of milk stable.

L: Are you sure about that?

E: I am absolutely sure about it.

M: You are proposing logic and common sense for everything then?

E: That would be correct. It's worth learning common sense in any situation. Would you really have it any other way?

I feel the time has come for us to finish this session. I hope that I've been as rational as possible and that I've provided you with a little insight about children.

L: I'd say you've cleared up a concept or two for us.

M: Yes, I agree. To end, could you offer an ABC plan, or other simple premise to follow?

E: That's fair, you've given me your undivided attention – I've devised a little outline that I hope will be useful. This is it:

"**P**" – **P**rep us with positive expectations and directions before we get started with anything.

"**O**"– **O**bject to the symptoms of our misdeeds, by

Objectively assessing behavior without biased judgment – see through to the abilities that generate our impulses.

"S" – Separate us from the action, and follow through on your promises, with time samples (clocks, calendars) and use consequences only as a Secondary measure for discipline.

"I" – Involve yourself in some of our play activities.

"T" – Teach & discipline without the uses of no, not, don't, can't, and shouldn't.

"I" – Implement common sense with relative effects or correlating consequences.

"V" – Variety across the board will keep us from becoming *bored.* New activities and different ways to do them will keep us stimulated and help us develop creativity; a necessary element for fulfillment (diversification).

"E" – Empathize with us. The world is a confusing and complicated place. – And remember to take time to make observations and ask questions as much as possible!

L: That sums it up quite well.

E: I appreciate the time you've spent here with me listening to my concerns. I'd like to conclude by including a note of recognition and praise to anyone who has refused to accept adversity and strife as part of their destiny. To those folks who have strived to create and recreate themselves in their own worthy images – Thank you for your efforts, examples and contributions in the world of human development. I wish you peace, love and creative fulfillment.

M: Will we ever meet again?

E: We'll all meet again, I'm sure of it. So long!

L: Goodbye Eve.

PART THREE

INTRODUCING THE FORMAT AND SEMANTICS OF COGNITIVELY - CORRECT™ LANGUAGE; THE POSITIVE DIALECT

The following section is a sample compilation of phrases that constitute the type of guidance and speech that is characteristic of Cognitively-Correct™ language.

It is vital that you challenge literacy about the knowledge of potential. To offer an example, the first suggestion in the first section on Safety, Health and Hygiene proposes that you offer an option for your child's natural curiosity to explore the world. This is unconventional and even daring where safety is concerned. Often (as has been challenged in current and past seminars) is the objection that, a child will - and has - met this curiosity issue with finding a chair of suitable height that would allow him to view the top of the stove himself. There are several ways to alter or address such a command that still meets the true premises of a language that proposes ability, capability, trust, competence, creative development and diversification. These are the main traits of the dialect standards for the knowledge of potential.

To return to the example, telling your child that he can see the top of the stove only if you pick him up - can be used as a literal command.

If your child is creative and curious enough to devise his/her own way to see the stove, by standing on a chair or climbing the counter, it is up to you to be aware of your own child's abilities and re-create directions that still include: encouraging your child's creative abilities and advantages in other areas (while you insist on absolute compliance with safety rules), promises fulfilled and realized (one day he or she will be able to see the stove by themself and certainly have a better idea about safety at that time or stage), your trust in them to be able to follow specific, constructive directions for this or any other functional area of development.

Remember, the ultimate purpose of Cognitively -Correct™ speech is to help you develop a literacy for the knowledge of potential, benefits, advantages, possibilities, abilities, talents, trust, competence and confidence - because that is how we truly learn and advance.

To literally and truly explain preschool development would require having ten voices to speak about all functions of development at the same time and for the listener to have ten pairs of ears to process all the interconnecting information at the same time. This is what makes preschool development virtually inconceivable to convey. However, since all things are virtually possible, this manuscript has been created to assist you on your own literacy into the knowledge of potential and the possibilities you can imagine and realize for yourself and the children you love and care for.

XI

HEALTH, SAFETY HYGIENE

XI HEALTH, SAFETY & HYGIENE	
Cognitively-Correct™:	*Cognitively-incorrect:*
Please keep your distance from the stove, it is very hot. I can pick you up if you'd like to see the top. When you are taller than the stove you'll be able to see it yourself.	Don't touch the stove.
Wet your hands first, then put soap on your hands and rub them together until you make lots of bubbles, the more bubbles you make the cleaner your hands will be. After that, be sure to rinse away all the bubbles with plenty of water until your hands sound squeaky clean.	Wash you hands properly. (z) You didn't wash your hands well enough.

XI HEALTH, SAFETY & HYGIENE

Cognitively-Correct™:	Cognitively-incorrect:
You can use a small butterknife at dinnertime while I oversee / watch you. For now, let's find another tool that you can use. Would you like some plastic spoons and paper plates to play with? (z) To use with your playdoh™ or clay? (y) To make mud-pies in the backyard? (x) Later when we have a snack, you can spread your own peanut butter on your crackers.	You can't play with the knife. (z) You can't use a knife for anything, (y) You'll just make a big mess, I'll do that for you.
You have plenty of play pillows and blankets. Clean sheets are only for the beds. Please put them away and help me remake this bed.	You can't take those clean pillows and blankets off the bed to play with.
If you want to jump, you'll have to go outside or wait until we get to the park. If the bed was built to be a trampoline, then I'd let you jump on it, but it is designed for sleeping, for laying down, and remaining very still.	Don't jump on the bed, you'll fall and crack your head.
We cross the street together. (z) We only cross the street or parking lot when we're together and holding hands with an adult.	Don't cross the street by yourself. (z) Don't you dare go out in the street by yourself.
Stay away from the pool. Stay with me until were all ready to go together. Those are the rules, we never go in the pool alone or without supervision.	Don't go in the pool yet. (z) You can't go in yet. (y) I said you can't go without me, just wait.

XI HEALTH, SAFETY & HYGIENE	
Cognitively-Correct™:	*Cognitively-incorrect:*
As soon as you're buckled up, we'll be ready to go.	We're not going anywhere until you're buckled in the car seat.
If you want to throw something go outside and throw a ball around. Throwing is an outside activity. Your choices for inside play include; block building, house play, using legos™, puzzles, etc. Sports and ball playing are strictly for outside, leave the ball by the door so you know exactly where it is when you're ready to go out again.	Don't throw anything. (z) If you keep throwing that thing and something breaks you're going to get punished, and I won't take you anywhere later.
The stairway is for the use of walking up and down, you can climb the monkey bars at the park when we go this afternoon. If you have that much energy go outside and run around for a few minutes.	You can't play on the stairs. (z) Don't play on the stairway.
If doors were toys, then you could play with them, there are doors on your play-trucks / doll houses to play with. But doors we use to go in and out of are heavy and can move very fast. You could get something caught in it, like your favorite toy. If your finger got caught in it, we'd have to go the emergency room and then you'd lose your playtime. [-a natural consequence]	Don't play with the door. (z) Get away from the door. (y) The door is not a toy. (x) You'll get your fingers caught.

XI HEALTH, SAFETY & HYGIENE	
Cognitively-Correct™:	**Cognitively-incorrect:**
Playing on or near the window is absolutely off limits. If you really want to look out the window, please tell me and I'll hold you while we look out together.	Don't go near the window.
It's better to play in the rain in the summertime when the rain is warm. Right now the rain is too cold – when it's wet and cold we have to dry up to avoid catching colds. That's why we take warm baths. If you want to take your bath earlier tonight, you can have a longer bathtime, so you can play with water. (z) If it means that much to you, put all your raingear on and dress warmly, you've got 10 minutes.	No, you can't go out in the rain you'll get sick.
Never speak to strangers unless I am with you. If a stranger talks to you, please ignore them and stay close by me when we are in public areas. If a stranger ever asks you for help when you are outside playing, you must come inside immediately and speak with me right away.	Don't ever speak to strangers. You don't know who they are, and they could be bad or want to hurt you.[1]
We must follow the doctor's direction for taking this medicine. The medicine is to help your body get better. When you're feeling better then you can have some candy.	No, you can't have another spoonful the medicine is not candy.

XI HEALTH, SAFETY & HYGIENE

Cognitively-Correct™:	Cognitively-incorrect:
If you really dislike the taste of the medicine then you can eat it with something that you really like.	It doesn't matter if you don't like the taste of the medicine, you have to take it or you won't get better.
The chair is for sitting the floor is for standing. We sit while we're eating. The sooner you finish eating the sooner you can leave the table. You'll have to stay here until you're finished.	Don't stand on the chair, you'll fall and crack your head.
You can have dessert when you've finished all of your dinner.	You can't have dessert unless you finish eating all your dinner.
You know the rule, if you eat all of your dinner, you can have a serving of ice cream, if you want a second helping of dessert, you can have a second helping of dinner first.	No, you can't have more ice cream. (z) If you're still hungry, eat some more dinner.
You can choose something from another food group. You've already had that food group today.[1]	You already had too much junk food today. (z) You can't have more junk food, you didn't eat enough nutritious food today (y) Have something that's good for you.[2]

XI HEALTH, SAFETY & HYGIENE

Cognitively-Correct[tm]:	Cognitively-incorrect:
Sand is for fun and playing, if you must throw, then get out of the sandbox and throw a ball. The sand can never be used for throwing. You can make sand castles or dig with a shovel, collect some in a jar, you can even roll around in it, if you throw sand or the shovels or pails, we'll go home. (z) If it gets in your eyes, it will be very uncomfortable or hurt.	Don't throw sand, it could get in someone's eyes and that would be bad, because you can really hurt someone. (z) If you do it again, I'll take away one of your privileges.[3]
Sticks are for digging or making things. You can use it to make designs in the sand, or to dig for worms. You have one chance to use it creatively and properly. If you use it to poke some-one or if you throw it, we will leave immediately.	Don't poke or hit anyone with sticks . (z) If you do that again, you'll get a time out.[4]
I understand if you dislike brushing your teeth, but if you want to be able to eat candy, you have to have strong healthy teeth (z) Lots of people dislike brushing their teeth. There are lots of things we'd like to avoid doing because they are unpleasant. Let's think of something to make it easier. 1-Would you like me to keep you company? 2- Would you rather sit down on your stool instead of standing up? 3-Do you want to put your favorite music tape on while you brush?	It doesn't matter if you don't like brushing your teeth, you have to brush them whether you like it or not / If you don't brush your teeth you can't have candy.

XI HEALTH, SAFETY & HYGIENE

Cognitively-Correct™:	Cognitively-incorrect:
Let's see you brush each and every tooth. If you want to eat candy, you've got to have healthy teeth, so you can chew on it.	You call that brushing your teeth, you had the toothbrush in your mouth for two seconds. (z) Brush your teeth properly or they'll fall out.
We only eat one sweet per day (z) Friday is our candy eating day (y) We only eat sweets on family outings (x) Tomorrow we'll have plenty of candy for your birthday party.	Don't ask me to buy you candy, you can't live and grow on junk food (z) We're not buying candy (y) I just said "no", stop asking.
Please use a washcloth to scrub yourself, it's the best way to get off all the dirt. Do you want me to help you or do you want to do it by yourself?	You didn't wash yourself properly, there's still dirt all over, you didn't use any soap.
Finish scrubbing yourself clean, make lots of bubbles. When you're done then you can play with the soap (z) It's time to get out now, tomorrow you'll have another chance to play in the bath.	You can't stay in the bathtub all night just playing, you've got to clean yourself and get out.
If you sit down in the bath tub, you can stay longer and play. If you stand up that means you're finished bathing.	Don't stand in the bathtub, you'll fall and crack your head.
I know you are a big girl, but we sit when we take a bath and we stand when we take a shower, which do you prefer?	If you stand in that bathtub once more, I'll get you out and you'll go straight to bed. (z) If you keep standing it'll serve you right if you slip and fall.

XI HEALTH, SAFETY & HYGIENE	
Cognitively-Correct™:	*Cognitively-incorrect:*
If you're thirsty, I'll get you a cup of water, the bath water is dirty and it has soap in it, it could cause a tummy-ache.	Don't drink the bath water that's disgusting, it's dirty, do you want to get sick?
When we're in public we have to hold hands or stay close together, especially when there are lots of people around, it's possible to get lost in a crowd of people.	Don't wander away. (z) Don't wander around (y) Don't wander off without me, what if a stranger takes you away and you never see mommy again, huh?

A NOTE ABOUT THE FUNCTION OF SAFETY, HEALTH AND HYGIENE:

All cognitive functions depend on acquiring and learning advantages and benefits, especially with regard to the traits of unique talents and abilities.

However, the area of safety covers more urgent concerns. Therefore, it's quite natural to balance the knowledge of disadvantages or consequences about dangerous or unsafe situations, provided an equal coverage is given to the advantages of following safety precautions, and without the knowledge of fear and guilt.

In the case of other functional developments, that correlate directly with aptitudes and capabilities, it is always more advantageous to direct, teach and discipline based on the knowledge of possibilities and creative options.

COMMENTS AS QUESTIONS

HEALTH SECTION:

- Did you wash your hands properly by making lots of scrubbing bubbles before rinsing?
- Do we eat only junk food or lots of different types of food to help us grow?
- Would you like to have a second serving of dinner so you can have a second helping of dessert?
- Would you like to use a small butter knife to spread your own peanut butter?
- When you're done with dinner you can have dessert, how soon do you want to have dessert?
- Actually, today is Wednesday, do you remember which day is our candy-buying day?
- Why do we take medicine? (z) Is this candy or medicine? (y) Would you like me to read the doctor's directions on the label so that you know exactly what the doctor's directions are.

SAFETY SECTION:

- Are you allowed to touch the stove?
- Would you like some old sheets and pillows for your own play area?
- Do we cross the street alone or together?
- Are we allowed to go outside the fence without an adult or without permission?
- Have I mentioned that the stairs are only for going up and down and never to play on?

- Did you ask permission to open the window? (z) Is the window-sill one of the items from your toy chest?
- Are you allowed to speak with strangers unless I am with you by your side?
- Do we wander off alone or on our own, or do we stay alto-gether when we're in public places?
- Do we go out to play in the cold rain or the warm rain? (z) Do we go out in the rain to play without our rain gear?
- Do we stand or sit on chairs?
- Did I make it clear that we can never wave a stick around someone's face or throw it around?
- Are you standing in the tub because you're ready to get out of the bathtub?
- Can you show me how you buckle yourself up in the car seat, let's see how you do it? (z) Let's see it ~ do you realize you did that all by yourself?

HYGIENE SECTION:

- Did I say you could go ahead without me? (z) Did I mention that we never go in the water alone?
- Did you brush each and every tooth? Did you know that you have to brush each and every tooth for 5 seconds, can you show me how you did that?
- Did you know that we have to wait until you've brushed your teeth before we can have story time?
- Can you show me how you scrubbed each and every spot?
- Do you mean to tell me that you're thirsty?! - if so, please ask me to bring you some drinking water instead of drinking the dirty bath water?

THE HOW AND WHY OF COGNITIVELY CORRECT:

1. Have a food chart with food groups; proteins-meat and fish, fruits & vegetables, grains, dairy, and 'junk food', so that you can point out the options.

THE HOW AND WHY OF COGNITIVELY INCORRECT:

1. Avoid scaring children, find out from local authorities what kind of information they currently use to educate children about strangers or requests they make of children.
2. This is an example of something we assume children know or accept, educate without judgment – offer the options.
3. Remember consequences should correlate the behavior and it should be in the moment. If consequences happen later children will lack a reference.
4. Time-outs are better reserved for talking about the incident or for cooling off. Isolation creates more frustration than impression.

USEFUL MATERIALS / SUPPLIES:

✓ Homemade poster of general rules
✓ 5 food group chart
✓ Safety & First Aid items (fully stocked – ask your local pharmacist).
✓ Local Police station telephone number
✓ Fire Dept. telephone number
✓ Poison control center hotline number
✓ Next of kin/trustworthy neighbor telephone number
✓ Safety locks/latches

✓ Consider taking a Child or community CPR class and/or a First Aid class

Post or list any allergies family members have in the event of an emergency, including allergies to medications so that other caretakers have something to refer to.

~Keep in freezer, separate individual bags, labeled with the name of each child; one cotton swab sample of their saliva and one of their blood (from a cut or scrap), also a few strands of hair.

XII

LEARNING ENVIRONMENT

XII LEARNING ENVIRONMENT	
Cognitively-Correct™:	**Cognitively-incorrect:**
If you want to play with water you can help wash the dishes after dinner. If you'd really rather have water play right now I'll give you a couple of cups of water and you can go outside and play with it.(z) If you play with water in the bathroom sink, it gets everywhere because the sink is small, there's very little room to play, and the floor is very slippery when it's wet.(y) Since it's too cold to go outside, I'll give you a bowl of dry noodles or rice and a few cups to play with on the kitchen table. (x) Would you like to bring in a large bowl of snow and make snow cookies?*	Don't play with the water (z)You can't do the dishes, I have to make sure they're done properly. (y) Stay away from the sink, you'll get all wet (x) You're getting water everywhere.
Here's a sponge, when you're done cleaning just continue with what you're doing.	See what you did, you spilled it, I told you to be careful. (z) Why do you have to be so careless?

XII LEARNING ENVIRONMENT	
Cognitively-Correct™:	**Cognitively-incorrect:**
You can get dirty and play with dirt when you're dressed in messy play clothes. Today we have dress clothes on because we are going to visit your Grandparents for dinner. Please stay away from messy or dirty things for today.	Don't get dirty.
If you want to play with the mud, please put on some messy play clothes and I'll give you some supplies to make mud pies or to do some digging. We'll clean up when we're done.	Don't you dare get dirty or go near the mud and I don't want any dirt in the house either.
Please leave the dog's tail alone, if you want to play with the dog or pet him, please treat him with kindness and gentleness (z) Pet the dog gently.	Don't pull the dog's tail.
Please start cleaning your play areas, and put all your toys away, the sooner you're done the sooner you can have dessert so we can leave on time for your play date.	If you don't pick up your clothes and toys, then you won't have a snack, (z) won't go to your play date.
We have to leave in '5' minutes, I understand that you'd like to stay but we can come back another time. We'll set a date and write it on the calendar so you can see it.	No, we can't stay.

XII LEARNING ENVIRONMENT

Cognitively-Correct™:	Cognitively-incorrect:
Let's make your bed together, the sheets are large, it works better with two pairs of hands.	You can't make your bed like that, you did it all wrong.
Our candy day is on Friday, today is Tuesday, we'll be back on Friday to buy a few things for the weekend and we'll buy your choice of candy then.	We're not buying any candy today. Don't ask me again.
If you want to make a tent or play with pillows and blankets, I'll give you some old ones that you can keep and use for playing. You can have them as soon as you put the bedding back on the bed.	You can't take all the blankets and pillows off the bed just for play. (z) The bed covers are very expensive, they're not to play with.
The toilet is used for one thing and one thing only, it can never be used as a garbage or storage and definitely never to put toys or any bathroom items. You have a play area. The bathroom door is staying closed.	No, don't do that - that was a terrible thing to do, we don't put things in the toilet, do you want to cause a flood in the whole house?
If you want to play rough you can go outside to run and jump around. (z) Please use soft things to play rough, a small pillow or a piece of cloth without any buttons or zippers or hard pieces on it.(y) Please go to your play room / basement / outside.	Calm down and stop all that rough playing, someone will get hurt (z) Don't come crying to me when you crack your head open. (y) If you don't stop all that rough playing, I'm going to take all of your privileges away.

XII LEARNING ENVIRONMENT

Cognitively-Correct[tm]:	Cognitively-incorrect:
Please stop playing with your food. The food is to eat and we play with toys. (z) When we sit down at the table for a meal we eat and enjoy each other's company. When we do a cooking activity together, you'll have a chance to play with some of the ingredients.	Don't play with your food. (z) What do you mean you don't want to eat, be grateful you have something to eat, do you know how many starving children there are in the world?**
If it helps you to remember to use your napkin to wipe your hands, please hold it in one hand while you use the other to hold your fork (z) Please use your napkin.[1]	Don't wipe your hands on your clothes, show some appreciation, I work hard to buy you nice things, you're getting stains all over, it'll be ruined.
Use your fork to eat. (z) As soon as you're done eating, you'll have time to play again.	Don't wave your fork around like that, you'll poke someone's eye out. (z) If you wave that fork around once more, you're going to leave the table.
You understand that if you break your toy, it'll stay that way. Some things can be broken and easily fixed but other things will never be the same again. Let's get some cardboard that you can make something with or break it.	Don't destroy your toys. That was really expensive, I work very hard for my money, how could you do something like that? (z) I just got your that (y) I hope you learned your lesson!***
You can have your toy back as soon as you're finished eating . (z) You can put your teddy bear on a chair next to you while you eat.	Don't bring your toys to the table. (z) I don't want your stuff all over the table, leave it in your room.

XII LEARNING ENVIRONMENT

Cognitively-Correct™:	Cognitively-incorrect:
I'm sorry you broke your toy, maybe you were expecting something else to happen, let's see if we can fix it with some glue or tape. (z) There may be a chance that we can get you another one - if we do then you'll have to do your best to make it last and keep it in good condition.	That's too bad, there's no way you're getting another one of those trucks, do you have any idea how expensive that was? I'm really disappointed, you should have never destroyed that.
If you want to make room for new toys and things to play with, you have to put these things away. (z) Please put these things away so we can see where we're going to make room for your new toys.	I'm not ever buying you another toy until you clean up this mess, even when Christmas comes, if this mess isn't cleaned up, your new toys will go straight into the attic (z) I'm not doing your cleaning for you, get this mess cleaned up.
We can use and handle our own things/personal items - things we see outside are either public property or they belong to someone else.	Please don't touch everything you see. I told you to keep your hands to yourself.
You can only handle the tools when either Dad or I are with you to supervise- when you'd like to help us fix something. That's the only reason we take them out and use them. (z) The electric tools can be handled only by an adult. If you're that interested in tools, we'll find you a children's tool set that's all yours.	You've asked me a hundred times already and I said "no", what is it that you don't understand- you just can't play with the tools. Why do you keep asking for things that you can't have (z) you have plenty of things to play with, why did I spend money on good toys for you to ask me for dirty garage tools?

| XII LEARNING ENVIRONMENT ||
Cognitively-Correct™:	Cognitively-incorrect:
I'm sorry your play date cancelled today and that you're on your own, I understand that you're disappointed, would you like some time to be alone? (z) would you prefer to call someone else? Can I help you to get started doing something else? (y) --Of course I can play with you for a little while. Tomorrow we'll go to the park, maybe you'll make some new friends while we're there.	Things like that happen sometimes, what can I tell you, it's too bad - that's life! I wish I could help you out. I'm sorry your play date didn't work out but I still have things to do, I scheduled that play date so that I can get some work done, and so that you'd have something to do at the same time, but I still have work to do, so you're just going to have to play by yourself.
It's better to keep your belongings in some kind of order- dolls with dolls, blocks with other building things, this way they're easier to find next time you play. (z) You can have a star to put on your cleaning chart as soon as you're done.	What do I have to do to get you to clean up, huh? You call this a clean-up job, you can't just put things away like that – then I have to listen to you complain that you can't find anything.

COMMENTS AS QUESTIONS

MESSY AND WATER PLAY SECTION

- Do you want to play with some water outside or with some dry noodles inside?
- Would you like to help me with the dishes or would you rather wait until bath time to play with water?
- Do you want to have dirty play outside or messy play inside?

CLEANLINESS SECTION

- Would you like to have a snack as soon as you pick up your clothes? / Would you like to go for a walk after you pick up your clothes?
- Do you want me to bring you a cleaning rag or would you like to get it yourself?
- Would you like some help to make your bed? Do you want to try again, I'll keep you company while you get it done?
- Can you please put your room in order neatly and reserve a spot for the new things you'll be getting?
- How fast would you like to clean your room so that we can go and buy your own tool set?

MANNERS SECTION

- Could you please show me how you pet the dog gently?
- If there's something you'd like to play with aside from what's yours or among your personal belongings, then I'm reminding you that you have to ask for it.

- Can we please go over some ground rules about playing rough? Can you wait until we go to the park later to play rough? Do you need to run outside for a little while? Have you forgotten to ask me to stay with you for a few minutes while you play rough?
- Have you forgotten the rules about touching other people's personal things?

GENERAL SECTION

- Do you want some old pillows and blankets to play with? Some old clothes for a house-play activity?
- What do we use the toilet for? Do we ever use the toilet as a garbage can? Why did you put that in the toilet?2
- What are you doing with your food? Is the meal time for eating or playing? Could you please tell me what your fork is for?
- We only bring ourselves to the meal table, do you want to take that away or would you rather put it away yourself?
- Do you really want to cut your doll's hair off, or is it that you just want to do some cutting? Should we discuss that before you cut your doll's hair, just to be sure that it is the change you want to make?
- I see you made some changes on your doll / toy, are you happy with the change?3
- What did you learn from that experience? Did you learn something about making changes to your toys that are different from how you normally use them?

TIME AWARENESS SECTION

- I understand that you'd like to stay, would you like to come back sometime?

- Would you like me to put a reminder on the calendar, or write you a note – for our candy buying day / our trip to the zoo / your birthday party / the time we'll be leaving for our vacation? [4]

THE HOW AND WHY OF COGNITIVELY CORRECT

1. Getting into the habit of doing things "right" is a matter of time, reminders and experience.
2. This can be tricky if children have watched you flush hair or old refrigerator food down the toilet. Toilet latches and supervision may be your only allies.
3. Is it necessary to put any ideas in their mind that they'd be 'ruining' their belongings or toys? In their mind they may just be experimenting or making a change. Perhaps the idea of it being ruined provokes the notion that it may have to be replaced?
4. If it's written somewhere, rather than them 'ask' you incessantly, they'll 'tell' you periodically. Literacy is based on and built in purpose. The time and care taken to put something in writing has little to do with their ability to read yet. It is giving credibility to their personal concerns and contributes to their inclination for participating and fitting into the scheme of events in their environment. The seemingly insignificant task of writing something specifically for their purpose gives children a chance to learn 'delayed gratification', because they would have a substantial reminder that gives them a sense of security. When promises are fulfilled, then the knowledge for delaying gratification can become a natural acquisition. By the same token, as life would have it, there are times when things change or events cancel beyond our control. As part

of children's learning functions such as dealing with disappointments, you might take a few moments to sit together, ask questions and write – taking a precise, exact dictation regarding their feelings about a disappointment, without judgment. This quality interaction will strengthen your bonds, elicit trust, and acceptance by exhibiting how important their feelings are to you too as much as they are to them. Interactions such as these help children process difficulties.

USEFUL MATERIALS / SUPPLIES

✓ Building blocks, large and small age appropriate toys,
✓ old blankets, pillows, scarves,
✓ plastic – funnels, cups, bowls and bottles (small).
✓ Old pots and pans – outside play (cover with a towel to use as a 'drum set' for inside play),
✓ music for dance and movement, instruments,
✓ water play items for outside –water slide, sprinkler, pails.
✓ Bath time toys.
✓ Used milk containers for mud play or planting seeds.
✓ Paper towel / toilet paper – cardboard center for imaginary / creative play, messy play.
✓ Clear plastic soda containers (cut evenly and finished on trimmed edges with masking tape)—for catching fireflies, guppies, tadpoles, salamanders, worms, cicadas, sand, etc.).
✓ Small self-made decorated boxes for collecting.

* Snow cookies (Reduces winter cabin fever)

Materials;

Large bowl or 6" deep washing bucket.

Snow

Very small metal molds (can be purchased in any home and kitchenware store).

Dark chocolate.

Pure coconut fat.

Superfine sugar.

Vanilla extract.

Instant coffee. (Optional, but it's less caffeine than a coke and adds a delicious mocha flavor).

In a double boiler, melt 3 ounces of coconut fat with 1 tablespoon of superfine sugar. In a cup, mix 1 tablespoon of vanilla extract with 1 teaspoon of instant coffee. Stirring constantly, slowly add to coconut and sugar mixture. Add 8 – 10 ounces of dark chocolate. Keep stirring until all ingredients are well blended together. Turn off heat. (If you use 2 pots as a double boiler, be sure water level is low enough to avoid spilling into mixture, it will damage the smooth consistency). Fill bucket with snow. Remove chocolate mixture from stove. Wrap a kitchen towel around double boiler to protect children from burns. Place on hot pads in middle of table. Give each Child a spoon and a few molds. Supervise and coach children to fill each mold with chocolate and place them on the top of the snow gently pushing the molds slightly into the surface. Watch as they harden. Using the handle side of the spoon, carefully push chocolate mold out of mold casing and place them face up on a plate. Continue process until all the chocolate is finished. Place in refrigerator, eat, enjoy, or save for a family get-together.

APPENDIX A

**Remember that children have a hard time processing abstract ideas and if they are meant to feel ashamed for what they have, who they are, or what they do, guilt will prevent and/or cause difficulties when learning to make connections. There are all kinds of political climates and social issues that have caused world problems and children can never be made to feel responsible for things out of their control. When they are older, there will be time and opportunities to teach them about those things. In the meantime, monitor and modify the amounts of food you give them and take note of their growing spurts or changing tastes.

***Children need new experiences and few four-year-olds have had lessons on the values and rules of the money game. But wasting money or insulting your hard work has nothing to do with either their intentions or the equation. First of all, if you intend to give something to your children conditionally, then state your conditions upon giving it. However if you would like children to understand the difference between 'what's mine' and 'what's yours', then respect possession with some absolute boundaries. If what they have or own is all about your feelings instead of theirs, then how will they decipher feelings or respect about other people's things when ownership boundaries of their own possessions are contingent upon someone else's conditions? Unconditional receiving sets the template and pattern for unconditional giving. Denying a Child the full effects of enjoyment for receiving unconditionally is only going to impinge on your efforts to foster feelings of gratitude, as is causing them to feel ashamed about 'being grateful for what you got'. When you give, give without conditions. On the other hand, giving everything they want or ask for all the time without reservation will create self-absorbed individuals who eventually master the art of selfishness, in which the world revolves around them. If eventually you want them to fully initiate or fulfill their responsibilities, they must have a sense freedom for that responsibility or for being in charge of what's theirs. If the terms of their possessions are always left up to someone else, they will relinquish responsibility for them, because they have felt forced to relinquish ownership of things that supposedly belong to them. If the ultimate decision is going to be someone else's, what's the point? Even as children are dependent human beings, they believe they are becoming independent and that belief has to be fostered. 'Coach' children through the steps of caring for their environment. Young human beings are dependent on encouragement. How they become independent vessels of reciprocating good virtues will depend on how much they could depend on being dependent of receiving attendance to those virtues. Additionally, if you regard 'things' over their esteem, what do you think they'll do by the time they are teenagers when you want them to consider others feelings? If they put things over family values and quality time – they will have been doing exactly what you taught them.

XIII

PHYSICAL

XIII PHYSICAL	
Cognitively-Correct™:	*Cognitively-incorrect:*
I'll stand right next to you while you climb, only climb as high as I can reach up my hand ~ 'til here! That way I can help you get down if you need it.	Don't climb too high / I don't want you climbing too high. You might have trouble getting down.
I'll be right next to you if you want to hang upside down for 5 or 10 seconds.	Don't hang upside down like that, all the blood will go rushing to your head.
It is absolutely forbidden to climb on anything inside the house. If you want to do some real climbing we'll find some activities outside for you to do. Find something to do that requires you to sit or stand, or walk inside the house. If you need help with this rule, I will choose something for you / Please play at the kitchen table, where I can see what you're doing.	Are you nuts, you can't go climbing all over the furniture like that. If you climb on that dresser, you better not come running to me crying and screaming cause you're hurt / I don't want to know that you've broken a bone or you're bleeding, do you think I want to spend all night in the emergency room?

XIII PHYSICAL	
Cognitively-Correct[tm]:	*Cognitively-incorrect:*
Hanging is something we do outside or in the park. You'll have plenty of opportunities to do some hanging when we go to the park.[1]	You can't hang on the door or table/edge of the couch like that. If you ruin the furniture, you're going to be in some serious trouble.
Walk, we walk inside / Please walk / Stop running, and walk / Let's go outside for a while if you want to run / We only run inside if there's some kind of emergency.	Don't run! If you don't stop running, you'll be sent to your room for the rest of the day.
Your choices for inside play include, listening to music, dancing, doing artwork, sitting down games, watching a movie, playing with building blocks etc.	Don't jump around / Don't do that, find something to do / Stop jumping on the couch like that you'll put a hole in it.
If you'd like to sit all day we can find you something to do that requires sitting. Would you like to play with clay or with some cards or do some drawing or make cookies? (z) Do you want to do something together? (y) Are you tired? Do you want to take a nap?	You can't just sit around all day and do nothing. (z) What's the matter with you, stop being so lazy, you'll become part of the couch if you just sit around all day like that. (y) Stop day-dreaming and go play or do something, you haven't done a thing all day.
There's a difference between shouting and talking in a quiet tone of voice, shouting is fine to do outside, and inside we speak quietly.	If you don't quit shouting right now, I'm going to send you to your room. Stop shouting, you'll break someone's eardrums.

XIII PHYSICAL	
Cognitively-Correct™:	**Cognitively-incorrect:**
I'm sorry that I left this plastic bag near your play area, it was my mistake. (z) Whenever you see a plastic bag you can bring it to my attention so that I can put it away. (y) I can give you a plastic cup to play with but plastic bags are totally off limits. If you are ever near a plastic bag, please tell an adult to remove it and always keep it away from anyone's face.	Don't you dare ever play with plastic bags, or put things in your mouth like that. That's a very bad thing to do, if I ever catch you playing with a piece of plastic like that again, you're really going to get it.[1]
If you insist on playing with the dirt / rolling around in the dirt, you'll have to put on some messy play clothes. You're free to get as dirty as you want, but those are the only clothes you have to wear until we get home. (z) If you pour dirt all over your clothes, you'll have to take them off before we go inside the house. (y) You can run around the dirt all you like / play with it all you like - enjoy yourself. I'm sorry I forgot to put your messy play clothes on today / bring a change of clothes for you, I hope we remember for the next time!	No, that's dirty, that's no good, what ever gave you an idea to do something like that!? (z) Don't put dirt all over yourself (y) Don't get your clothes dirty, those are good clothes (x) Do you think I'm made of money and can just go out and get you something new to wear everyday? (w) Don't you dare get one bit of dirt on your clothes or shoes, if you do, I'm never taking you with me again anywhere, ever! (v) Can't you just stay clean for five minutes, why can't I ever take you anywhere without you turning into a big mess before we even leave the house. (u) Are you even capable of staying away from anything messy or dirty?
What did you do today – did you play running games or sitting games, climbing games.	Did you have a nice day? What did you do today?[2]

XIII PHYSICAL	
Cognitively-Correct^{tm}:	**Cognitively-incorrect:**
If you want to swing something around, I'll give you a ribbon or a scarf, or a piece of cloth without buttons or zippers or anything hard. Hard things are never meant to be used for swinging or tossing inside the house.	That's not a smart thing to do, what if you hit yourself or someone else. (z) How could you do that, you hurt her. (y) You see what happens when you don't listen, now you've hurt yourself.
Would it be easier for you to clean up with some music on? (z) You have ten minutes more to play until it will be time to clean up. (y) The T.V. is part of your playing activities. It has to be turned off just as your toys have to be put away. (x) As soon as you put everything away you can watch television for about 10 minutes before dinnertime/ride your tricycle in the yard. If you hurry, you'll have about 15 minutes.	What makes you think I'm going to let you listen to music or watch T.V. while you clean up, you have enough trouble focusing as it is. (z) Stop what you're doing right now and clean up. (y) No, you can't have anymore time to play, you've played enough today. (x) I'll send you to your room and you won't have another thing to do today, if you don't listen to me right now (w) You're crazy if you think I'm going to let you play for another minute.
Please keep your fingers out of small holes, even if they are on your toys. If some-thing is stuck inside let me know so that we can use a tool to get it out and most importantly to keep your fingers from getting stuck or hurt. (z) If you want to put something inside of your toys, you can have something soft like a cotton ball that will be easy to remove.	Don't do that, if you get your finger stuck in that hole, you'll get just what you deserve (z) I told you not to do that, if you do that again, you'll never see that toy again, I'll put it away for good, and that'll be the end of it. (y) Do you expect me to feel sorry for you, after I told you a hundred times not to do that. I hope you learned your lesson now that you're hurt.
Even though we'll be in Grandma's house, you still have to ask permission to touch things, is that understood?	You know Grandma doesn't like it when you touch everything, so when we go inside you better just sit still.

XIII PHYSICAL

Cognitively-Correct™:	Cognitively-incorrect:
If your fingers need something to do, there are plenty of activities to keep your fingers busy. Get your clay out, or we can make you a fresh batch of dough to play with. You can go out in the yard and poke holes in the dirt to look for worms. (z) Never poke someone in the face with your fingers.	See what you did, you just had to be stubborn and ignore me. (z) You just never listen, go ahead and keep doing that, so you can see what I mean, you always insist on learning things the hard way. (y) Don't poke others in the face. (x) I never taught you to do anything like that. I'm ashamed of you. If you do that again, I'm going to smack you.
I understand your love for music, but it still has to be on a low volume in-side. You have batteries in it so that you can listen to it loudly outside (z) Please use your headphones, the baby is sleeping. (y) You can listen to some soft music while you clean up.	Turn that music down, where on earth do you think you are, at a concert hall?(z) If you turn up that music that loud again, I'm going to take your CD player away. (y) No, you can't listen to music while you clean up. (x) You can't goof around whenever it's time to do your responsibilities, I'm not running an amusement park here.
We're only buying the things on this grocery list, would you like to hold the list and help me find these things or would you like to push the cart?(z) We only touch the things we're buying.	We're not buying that, put it back right now, stop bugging me. No, I'm not buying you anything, we just came in here to get milk and bread.

XIII PHYSICAL

Cognitively-Correct™:	Cognitively-incorrect:
Before we go into the store, please enjoy looking at all the things in the store, but remember to keep your hands off and only look. (z) If it's easier to remember, perhaps you can put your hands in your pockets / hold your teddy bear so your hands have something to do. (y) We only touch things that belong to us. After I've paid for our new clothes, you can touch them all you like - once we get in the car / we're on our way home. (x) If you remember to keep to your hands to yourself, I'll give you the money to pay for the items at the counter.	Don't touch anything. (z) Keep your filthy hands off everything, do you think anyone wants to buy something you've put your dirty hands all over. (y) If I have to buy that thing because you dirtied it or damaged it, I won't buy you a thing for Christmas / your Birthday. (x) Don't even think about touching that or I'll smack your hand and we'll go straight home. (w) If you touch another thing in this store, you're going to get a time out when we get home, and we won't stop for any treats.(v) If you don't listen to me, I'm going to take away one of your privileges.
You can wash your hands and then have a cookie. (z) The rules about eating with clean hands have always been the same / have never changed. Put the cookie down and go wash your hands. (y) I know you washed your hands an hour ago / five minutes ago, but however many times we wash our hands, we still have to wash them again just before we eat anything.	Don't put your dirty hands in the cookie jar.(z) That's disgusting - do you think everyone else wants to eat dirty cookies just because you don't care if your own hands are dirty? (y) If you ever put your dirty hand in the cookie jar again you'll go to bed without eating a thing at all. (x) I don't care if you washed your hands before, you've been playing outside, they're filthy now.

XIII PHYSICAL

Cognitively-Correct™:	Cognitively-incorrect:
I've given you plenty of things that you have permission to cut. It's dangerous to put scissors anywhere near your head or face, that's why we go to the barbershop or salon. If you need something new to cut, please talk to me, I have ribbons and cereal boxes. (z) If you misuse your scissors again, we'll have to take away your cutting privileges for the rest of today. You can have another chance tomorrow after we go over the safety rules again. (y) Put the scissors down before you leave the table, using scissors is strictly a sitting down activity, and we only hold them when we're sitting down. (x) You can only run with something in your hand if its soft, like a bean bag or a ball.	Don't use scissors that way. You can't use your scissors to cut your hair, where on earth did you get the idea that you could cut your own hair? If you ever use scissors like that again, I'll put them away, and you won't get them back, ever. (z) Are you trying to get yourself killed, do you know how dangerous that is? (y) If you fall and stab yourself because you're running with scissors in your hand, you'll never touch another pair of scissors again.
Make a decision/choice - you can play inside or outside. Choose an activity, stick to it, clean it up and then move onto another activity. (z) If you start one thing and decide you'd rather do something else, first clean up and put it away and then start your next activity, this way when it's time to clean up, you'll only have one area to tidy.	You can't keep running inside and outside all day long. (z) You're making me dizzy running back and forth like this, I'm not running a carnival or three-ring circus here. (y) You're dragging dirt in the house, where do you think we live – on a farm? I don't have time to clean up this mess every five minutes.

XIII PHYSICAL

Cognitively-Correct™:	Cognitively-incorrect:
Everyone has to have some quiet time. I'll relax with you a little while, you try to rest. (z) If you have trouble sleeping, you can just sit quietly, lay down quietly on your bed and read a few books. (y) If you play and make noise during your nap/quiet time, then you'll have to get to bed earlier tonight so that you get enough sleep/rest. (x)Relax, and enjoy a little quiet time, that way you'll enjoy the rest of the afternoon without feeling tired. (w) If you stay awake for your entire naptime, you'll fall asleep earlier tonight and miss your favorite television program. (v) If you stay awake the entire time, you'll have to go to bed earlier tonight. (u) Please try to take a short nap, when you sleep that's when your body grows. If you rest, you'll be able to enjoy the rest of the afternoon without feeling tired, and you'll have more energy.	You can't skip your naptime, you have to go to sleep for a little while.(z) Don't have a little fit whenever it's time for you to take your nap. If you don't take a nap, you'll be miserable, and then I have to put up with your cranky, whiny attitude later on. (y) You have to go to sleep, otherwise later on you'll be nasty and cry about everything.[2]

COMMENTS AS QUESTIONS

LARGE MOTOR

- Do you want me to watch you climb, or do you want me to help you climb?
- Do you know the rules about running? Can you tell me where we're allowed to run?
- Are we allowed to throw anything inside? Do you remember the rules about throwing? Are we allowed to throw anything other than a ball?
- Do you remember the rules for inside play / for outside play? Are we allowed to climb on furniture or doors?
- What's the rule about running – with something in your hand? What's the only thing you can hold while you're running?

SMALL MOTOR

- Do you remember the rules about touching when we go inside a store? (z) Which things are we allowed to handle/touch in the store?
- Are you trying to build something new or are you trying to get something out of that small hole? Do you need help with that?
- Is there something you'd like to fix/did something of yours break?
- What are you doing with your fingers – are you trying to tell someone something? (z) Do you want to be alone for a while? (y) Do you want to go home now? (x) Do you know that it hurts when you poke someone like that?

GENERAL AND PLAY OPTIONS

- Are we supposed to bring dirt inside the house?
- How do we prepare for messy play / What's the first thing we do before we start messy play?
- Do you remember what I've told you about playing with plastic bags? (z) Did you know that you should tell an adult if a plastic bag is laying around?
- Why are you just sitting, do you feel tired / are you feeling sick? (z) Are you upset about something that someone did or said?
- Did you wash your hands? (z) What's the rule we follow before handling food or things inside the house-after outside play?
- How do we behave in the museum / in a public place?
- Would you like to listen to some soft music, or would you just like silence while you clean up?
- Did you listen when I gave you a ten-minute warning before it was time to clean up? Will you be ready to clean up in ten minutes?
- Do you want me to change your warning time to five minutes?
- How quickly can you get your cleaning done so we can move onto our next activity?
- Would you like to sleep or just relax quietly in your room? Did you know that you only grow while you're sleeping?
- Do you want to be awake later when it's time to watch your favorite T.V. program / when it's time to gather together for family evening play time/game time.
- Would you like to put on your raincoat and go outside for a walk, or would you rather stay inside and play? / Do you want to do something inside today or would you rather play in the backyard/at a friend's house?

- Would you like to do a cooking activity or a drawing/painting activity?
- You can play the music softly, or you can turn it off, which of those options/alternatives would you prefer?

THE HOW AND WHY OF COGNITIVELY CORRECT

1. If you Child is the kinesthetic type, and tends to center activities around large motor control movements, he may need extra chances to get out.

THE HOW AND WHY OF COGNITIVELY INCORRECT

1. Although it's easy to react about dangerous situations, children should never be made to feel guilty or responsible for things adults are supposed to watch out for.
2. This type of question is to vague for most preschool children, unless they are still excited or emotionally tied to the activity or have just broken away from it- or have a souvenir from a field trip, etc.
3. It's impossible to force someone to sleep, but you can enforce an atmosphere and limitations for activities and an environment.

USEFUL MATERIALS / SUPPLIES CHECKLIST

✓ Large and small balls for outside play
✓ Sponge/foam balls or bean bags for inside games
✓ Jumping ropes
✓ Trips to playground and water parks, museums, local nature tours (for hiking or to view waterfalls, caves, mountains, local features, etc.)

✓ Collect and explore different textures - their purpose and qualities, such as shiny, dull, soft, hard, rough, smooth / introduce mixtures – putting a recipe together, creating awareness about harmful elements (dirty water, poison ivy) Learn about useful/helpful materials such as spices, herbs, medicines/ointments

✓ Gather simple, small items from nature for creative use such as smooth stones for painting or to create an aquarium/rock garden. Collect leaves, sand or small pebbles to make collages.

✓ Fish with a net or catch butterflies with a net.

✓ For an evening family activity – catch fireflies in a jar.

✓ Apparatus/equipment for large physical movement such as tricycle, climbing bars, sitting skateboards, floor-level balance beam, large chalk pieces for drawing outside / time allocated for large and small motor activities.

✓ Plenty of playing balls –different sizes for different activities.

✓ Dressing themselves – making a choice between 2 appropriate outfits

✓ Putting on their own shoes

✓ Bubble wands

✓ Wading pools

✓ Old or re-decorated spray bottles (filled with water) for outside water play.

✓ Large cardboard boxes for inside and outside play

Please supervise children when they're using scissors, even though they are "Child-safe"

Use daily routines to help children learn to care for their environment and take control of their surroundings: Pouring their own milk or juice, disposing of trash, cleaning dirty dishes, allowing them the full enjoyment of making messes and cleaning them without micromanaging their processes either developmentally, intellectually, emotionally, physically (except where safety is concerned)

XIV

COGNITIVE

(MATH)

XIV COGNITIVE	
Cognitively-Correct™:	*Cognitively-incorrect:*
Did you bring your own money to buy that? (z) Unless you came with some money of your own, then please put it back. I only came with enough money to buy what's on our grocery list.(y) Would you like to help me out? – Here's the list of things we're buying today. Show me where you found that, let's put it back. (x) We can write that on our grocery list for our next shopping trip (w) Let's have a look at some of the other, similar products like that – there are better choices than that one. We'll find one that's suitable (v) The first thing on our grocery list is…	I'm not buying that for you, put that back right now, I don't have enough money to get that. (z) Don't ask me to buy you anything. (y) Don't touch anything, unless I tell you that you can have it. (x) I'm not buying anymore junk.(w) No, you can't have that. (v) That stuff is no good for you.

XIV COGNITIVE	
Cognitively-Correct™:	**Cognitively-incorrect:**
I gave you a 5 minute warning before to allow you time to finish your activity. You're 15 minutes are over, messy/creative play activities need extra finishing-up time, and it's time put these supplies away until tomorrow.[1]	Playing time is over, clean up right now. (z) No, you can't have 5 more minutes to play- you've had enough time as it is. (y) Just do as I say and don't argue with me. Just clean up right now.
Whichever way you practice writing numbers and letters is good practice.	That's the wrong way to write those numbers. You'll have to spend more time practicing.
We've had this discussion for a few weeks now, I've made it very clear what the rules/limitations are.(z) We'll have to create another type of reminder. I will write a note to be posted in that area / those areas - with your name on it, and the rule to follow until you remember on your own.[2]	I didn't say you could do that, I've told you "no" all along. If you do that again, I'll be really upset and mad with you. (z) I've told you that you can't do that, and that's that. If you do it again, you will be punished, that'll help you remember.
Let's see how many toys you can fit into each box/container until everything is put away.	I want to see this room sparkling in five minutes. (z) Don't leave anything lying around.
You can play with some things from the pantry.	You can't play with those things.
She's likes talking sometimes.	She doesn't like to talk much.
He does a good job trying to tie his own shoes.	He doesn't know how to tie his own shoes yet.
Just take two or three please.	You can't take that many.

XIV COGNITIVE	
Cognitively-Correct[tm]:	**Cognitively-incorrect:**
Money has to be earned - it takes time and work to make money. (z) Money is used as an exchange. It's similar to trading something.	I'm not made of money. (z) Money doesn't grow on trees. (y) I can't buy you everything you see.
That's very imaginative, but the way it really works is like this... (z) It's going to be difficult to get it done that way, but we could try this... (y) That actually belongs... it's purpose is to/for... (x) Just about anything is possible! (w) Tell me your ideas, I'll write them down in your journal.	That's ridiculous, things don't work like that. (z) It's impossible to get it done like that – you can't do it like that. (y) You'll never get it done that way. (x) That doesn't belong there. That's not supposed to be used like that. (w) Well, maybe it's a good idea, but I don't think it will work - we'll talk about it another time.
Do you mean this... or that...?(z) Are you trying to tell me that you dislike /prefer...? I'm sorry I misunderstood you. (y) Perhaps we'll try it that way next time.	I don't understand what you're saying, that doesn't make any sense. (z) Now's not a good time to start changing things around – you should have told me before.
Each thing has a sequence or pattern or steps to follow, try doing that in a different order, put this first...then that one second...	That doesn't go like that, you've got it all wrong. Do it right, you should know that by now. I don't have time to watch every little thing you're supposed to do.
Try doing that again.	You're doing that the wrong way.
That's a centipede, you see it has '100' short legs, a spider has '8' long legs.[6]	That's not a spider. That's a centipede.
We have a tight schedule today, we can only do one of these activities and tomorrow we can do the other one, which do you prefer to do today?	We can't do both things -make a choice (z) We can only do one of those activities depending on what I get done- I'll let you know.[1]

XIV COGNITIVE	
Cognitively-Correct™:	Cognitively-incorrect:
Let's look at the clock, I'll show you what it's going to look like when it's time to go – we have to wait for one more hour.	When it's time to go I'll let you know, just keep yourself busy until then. (z) We're not leaving yet.(y) It won't be for another hour or so.
Let's put a circle on the calendar so you can see what day we're leaving for vacation and how many days until then. Every morning you can cross out that day's number of the month.	You keep asking me that everyday. We're not going until next week, I keep telling you that, don't keep asking me (z) I told you when we're leaving, now give it a rest.
Can you guess what we're having for dinner? (z) Would you like cold salad or warm veggies with your dinner?	What do you want to have for lunch–and don't say pizza, cause we don't have it.
Do you want hamburgers or chicken for lunch?	When it's time to go I'll let you know, just keep yourself busy until then. (z) We're not leaving yet.(y) It won't be for another hour or so.
Do you want a big/whole sandwich for lunch or a little/half sandwich and some soup? (z) We have a limited choice, I'll shop tomorrow.	I'll make you something good to eat. (z) You'll just eat what I give you. (y) I haven't had a chance to shop, there's no food in this house.
Guess again, I'm sure you know the name of that shape.	No, that's not a square (z) that's wrong, you know the name of that shape, it's a rectangle.

XIV COGNITIVE

Cognitively-Correct[tm]:	Cognitively-incorrect:
The difference between circles and ovals are that one is completely and evenly round and the other is 'lop-sided' round. (z) The difference between squares and rectangles is that the square's lines are the same size on all sides and rectangles have two long sides and two shorter sides.[4]	Those shapes are not the same. They're similar but they're not the same.[3] (z) Squares and rectangles are not the same, you have to look at them more carefully. (y) You're not thinking, concentrate on it.
There's more than that, let's count together while we point to each one. There's less than that, let's count... 'Four' is this many, and seven is this many.[5]	You counted wrong. You have to get it right. (z) You're not counting carefully. (y) You're not paying attention to what you're doing.[4]
We'll go shopping first, return home and put the groceries away. Then we'll go to the park afterwards.	We've got other things to do. -- I'm not going to spend the whole day at the park / Stop bugging me or we're not going anywhere at all.
I'm sorry you really dislike food shopping. If you help me look for and gather all the groceries we need, we'll finish faster. (z) Everybody has things to do that they dislike, we just have to get through the things we dislike as quickly as possible so that we can spend more time doing the things we like to do. Life is like that for everybody.	Life just doesn't work that way, we have to do a lot of things we don't like. (z) It doesn't matter if you don't like shopping, I can't leave you home all alone. (y) You have to come with me whether you like it or not.

XIV COGNITIVE

Cognitively-Correct™:	Cognitively-incorrect:
Do you need help deciding what to do, shall we take a look around (z) would you like me to write a list of activities that you can choose from, we'll post it in your play area. (y) Would you like something new to do? – finger paint with pudding /whipped cream?	You can't just wander around and do nothing. Go play or something. (z) You have plenty of things to do, how can you tell me that you have nothing to play with. (y) I'm sure you can find something to do.
You can come in the kitchen if you stick to one project and finish it from beginning to end. – Would you like to make some cookies, or help me mix a cake? (z) You can keep me company in the kitchen but you have to do an activity at the table while I cook. Stay away from the hot stove.	You can't hang around the kitchen, there's hot food cooking on the stove. You can come in the kitchen for '5' minutes, but don't go near the stove. You know I don't want you in the kitchen when I'm cooking.
You can borrow my calculator for a little while and you can have one piece of computer paper and a pencil, sit at your table and make a work-station for yourself. Please return my calculator to my desk when you're done, so that you can have the privilege of using it again.	You can't just help yourself to my workspace, these things are too important for you to play with.[5]

XIV COGNITIVE

Cognitively-Correct™:	Cognitively-incorrect:
Please ask about things you want / want to do. (z) Please ask if you can have time / permission to do that now. We have other things to do first.(y) Did you put your toys away? You still have to take a nap or have some quiet time (x) Let's sit down and talk about a few options for the rest of the day.	Don't tell me what to do. (z) Do you expect me to just drop what I'm doing so that I can just do exactly what you want whenever you demand it? --What do you think I am? --Do I look like a maid? (y) Stop harassing me and go play quietly somewhere for a little while.
I'll help you with this, and then you can do the rest by yourself. (z) I'll help you put your shirt on and you can put your pants on by yourself. (y) Please help me to put away these things. –I'll put the dishes away and you put the pots and pans away.	You don't need my help, you can get that done on your own. (z) I'm not helping you, I have enough of my own things to do.(y) I don't need your help, you might break a dish, I will put them away myself.
I need to find a glass jar of jam, it has a picture of strawberries on it, can you help me? That's a tin can of peaches.	That's not jam, those are peaches, can't you see? You just have to look at it, there's nothing wrong with your eyesight, is there?
I told you that you could have a snack /treat *after* you put your shoes away. Put the treat down and get that done, then come back and finish your snack.	I didn't say you could have that snack before you put your shoes away, now you're not going to have a snack at all, go to your room.

XIV COGNITIVE

Cognitively-Correct™:	Cognitively-incorrect:
I told you that you could stay up for '10' more minutes if you put your pajamas on first. The next time you disregard our agreement, it'll be a couple of days before you have another chance for extra time, get ready for bed right now.	I get so mad when you don't listen to me. Bad boys don't get special treatment. (z) That's it, no more staying up late. You really hurt my feelings when you take advantage of my kindness like that.
Please sit down and do some drawing and scribbling. You have to spend a little time doing a sitting down game or activity.	You better sit down and do some practicing with your numbers and letters, and I'm going to be checking it, so do it "right".
Bring your tricycle in, put it in the garage, and put your muddy shoes in the laundry room.(z) Could you please repeat what I just asked you to do? – After you're done with that you can have a treat.	I didn't say that it was okay for you to leave your tricycle outside, don't put words in my mouth. I told you to put it in the garage, and don't you dare bring those muddy shoes inside the house. Why should I bother giving you a snack now?
What do you think will happen if you do that again?	You're just going to create a disaster if you do that.
What do you think will change if you pour water in your rice-playing tray, what will happen to the dry rice? You can mix water with pebbles or mud outside.	You're going to ruin it if you put water in there. I'm not cleaning it out and putting more rice in there every time you decide to put water in it.
Did you notice any changes in the window plants since a few days ago?	Look, there's a flower growing in this plant.

XIV COGNITIVE	
Cognitively-Correct[tm]:	**Cognitively-incorrect:**
Right now it's 2:30 in the afternoon, we'll rake leaves for now and later at 3:00 o'clock, we'll stop to have some hot soup - let me show you on the clock.	We'll have something to eat later, help me with this for now.[6]
Let's mark your measuring chart to see how tall you are / how much you've grown. The more nutritious food you eat, the faster you'll grow.	You're getting bigger (z) You're not going to grow unless you eat your vegetables.
If you want to play with cutlery I'll give you a small cup of flour and a plastic spoon after dinner so you can make patterns and designs on a paper plate or mat/ plastic table cloth. The table cutlery is strictly for eating our meal.	Don't scrap the fork and spoon on my good dishes (z) Stop playing with the silverware. (y) This isn't a band-practice session. I just want to have peace and quiet now. Just be still and eat your dinner.
I understand that you want your friends to use good manners, but when you've borrowed or taken something from someone, you must return it when you're finished using it. If someone took something of yours, you'd want that person to return it without you having to ask for it back. But if they ask for it back before you're finished, it would be the right thing for them to say, "May I please have my toy back now"? --And you should do the same thing if you lent something of yours to someone else. But it's okay to remind them.[7]	You can't take his things from him and then make him say please when he wants to have them back. (z) It doesn't work that way, you have to give that back to him, those are his belongings, it doesn't matter if he says please or not, you just have to give it back.

XIV COGNITIVE

Cognitively-Correct[tm]:	Cognitively-incorrect:
I understand that you want him to use good manners and say please, but he's just a baby and he's still learning to make sounds, it's too difficult for him to pronounce whole words yet. When you were a baby I gave you whatever you needed, then when you started learning how to speak, then you learned how to say please. (z) When you're finished using someone else's belongings, you should return it and say, "Thank you for letting me use your toy".	No, you can't do that, he's just a baby. He doesn't know how to talk yet. It's not yours, it's his, give it back to him right now. He doesn't know how to say please yet / You can't expect him to talk, you should know better. (z) Give it back to him right now or you'll get a time out when we get home. (y) You can't just take other people's things and then expect them to say please in order to get their own things back.
We only use the glass-measuring cup for baking and cooking. You can use the plastic-measuring cup to play. *For example, those times you are being asked the unusual, unreasonable or unexpected;* ☺ Yes, I know you are willing and able to clean it up if it falls and breaks, but we only have one glass-measuring cup, also when glass falls it shatters and scatters like heavy rain. It's extremely difficult to see where every piece goes and later on, a small piece that was hiding during the clean-up could get into someone's foot. (z) Yes, I know we still have a plastic measuring cup in case the glass one breaks, but we need the glass one for hot food or liquids, the plastic one would melt if we poured something hot in it.	No, you can't play with the glass-measuring cup. That's my good glassware. I don't spend my hard-earned money on good things so you can break and ruin them. (z) You can play with it for 5 minutes, but if you break it, then that will be the last time you'll ever use something of mine.[7] (y) It doesn't matter if you are willing to clean it up. I don't care about that. You just can't play with the glass one. Play with the plastic one or you can just forget about playing with either of them.

XIV COGNITIVE	
Cognitively-Correct™:	**Cognitively-incorrect:**
Yes, I noticed also that some people cross the street when the light is red, but it's safest to cross the street when the light is green, and *we* always prefer to do the safest thing – right?	Well, they're not supposed to do that. I don't ever want to see you do something just 'cause someone else does. Just because someone jumps off a cliff doesn't mean you would too!
That was very observant of you. Thank you for noticing that the car window was open when it started to rain. Let's get an umbrella and go outside and close it.	That was really a dumb thing to do. [8]
Yes, I know I allowed you to listen to loud music this morning, but we observe a quiet-play-time rule for the afternoons. Please lower the volume of the music.	You can't listen to loud music now, it's not a good time, there's a lot going on, just turn it down.
Yes, I know we are supposed to eat our meals when they are hot, but we have to wait for the cake to cool before we put icing on it, otherwise it will drip off / It will break if we take it out of the pan when it's still hot.	We can't eat the cake when it's hot. It's not the same, we are supposed to eat our food when it's hot, but you can't eat hot cake or you'll get sick.[9]

COMMENTS AS QUESTIONS

COMPARISON / MATH CONCEPTS

- Do you want your bath water a little warm or very warm?
- Do you want to put your new toy in the toy box or on the toy shelf?
- You have a choice of playing with a cardboard food container from the pantry and a plastic bottle from the container drawer, or I can help you get started with one of your own activities, but the glassware is off limits. Those are your choices, which do you prefer?
- Can you please show me your best table manners?
- Would you like me to count with you, or would you like to try counting on your own?
- Can I please hear you ask me that instead of telling me that? Would you like me to help you start the sentence correctly? – Mommy, may I please…?
- Where does your tricycle belong?
- Would you like to practice writing letters and numbers or do you prefer to just draw in your coloring book?
- Would you like to try again?

DECISION MAKING

- Would you like to help me push the shopping cart?
- Would you like to hold the grocery list?
- Do you want to play by yourself today or do you want me to call a friend?
- Do you want to do something new?
- Did you forget where that belongs?

- Would you like to help me put the groceries away?

THE HOW AND WHY OF COGNITIVELY CORRECT

1. If you're just beginning this practice, it'll take time to get used to, and you will probably meet with more resistance in this area then others for a couple of weeks until the idea is realistic, use the timer, or let them wear your wrist watch for the fifteen minutes.

2. Make rules personal, notes are effective and add purpose to their literacy development. If they bypass, forget or ignore the note, just point it out and ask them to remind you what the note states.

3. Remember to offer alternatives instead of the vague "what" do you want to drink?

4. Use evidence that's around you - draw, play "I spy" – to point out shapes or whatever else you're teaching with fun and games. Differences imply separate, distinct qualities, all of equal value. During this age of discovery and exploration, nothing is wrong, everything is a good guess that is reiterated or clarified with some specification.

5. Use fingers or objects, preferably something they are interested in.

6. That's math for a preschooler! If you want to be involved and hands-on and help them develop strong fundamental math skills, cut up little pieces of paper and put '100' then '8' in separate piles, or gather fallen leaves or use grains of rice or noodles, etc., be creative. There are many math concepts at work here; numbers, amounts, comparison, sorting, length, size. Exploration activities such as this one that involve many math concepts strengthen problem solving skills and the ability

to create solutions. By breaking down variables with examples, the abstract becomes concrete to the preschool mind. Hands-on demonstrates evidence that is visibly conclusive.

7. The dynamics of manners and social interactions are still experimental and very relative to young children. It's better to watch and observe how they work it out, and only interfere if distress arises.

THE HOW AND WHY OF COGNITIVELY INCORRECT

1. Uncooperative behavior you'd rather avoid when you're busy is forthcoming with this mysterious comment to the preschool mind.

2. Avoid teaching children to freely choose meals. Leave that for snacks and treats.

3. Similar and same are too much of a fine line for this concept.

4. If they're just playing, let them count any way they want, chances are they just want to have fun and hear themselves count.

5. Important might be the attraction, if your belongings are that important, close them off or make them "off limits", and respect their things equally.

6. Now and late' is fine, but it's still vague - specific is better, reverse activity and eating time if they're super hungry.

7. What are the chances? – that's a perfect set-up for a negative confrontation. Be tough, strict ruling is good here.

8. An ounce of prevention is worth a ton of treatment, but once something's done, propose the solution, avoid insults towards yourself or your children.

9. Make sense and make relative references - that's what makes math practical.

USEFUL MATERIALS / SUPPLIES CHECKLIST

✓ Toy cash register

✓ Play money / Homemade money*

✓ Large dice

✓ Dominoes

✓ Small variety-colored blocks

✓ Toys that match or fit

✓ Lis' of guessing games

✓ Play observation games;

✓ bird watching /bird listening,

✓ count seconds together while watching the second-hand move on a clock,

✓ watch and listen to a thunder and lightening storm – count seconds between lightening and thunder sound (covers science and nature learning skills, may help relieve fear of thunder through knowledge)

✓ Blind-fold identification – put different textured items in a box or bag and identify through touch and smell, or taste using different foods.

✓ Card games

✓ Matching games

✓ Hunting for hidden objects / Treasure hunts

✓ Timing games

✓ Word guessing games (Describing objects)

✓ Movement games – following multiple directions

✓ Tracing paper – for copying simple objects or shapes (drawn in bold black outlines)

* Cut and color paper, cover 1"–1 ½" size buttons with tin foil or cut round pieces of cardboard and color with metallic pens.

XV

COMMUNICATION / LITERACY / DEVELOPMENT / LANGUAGE ARTS

XV COMMUNICATION / LITERACY DEVELOPMENT / LANGUAGE ARTS

Cognitively-Correct[tm]:	Cognitively-incorrect:
Please use words that express exactly what you mean – I'll gladly help you with new words. (z) I understand that you heard a friend use that word, but it is their parent's job to help them understand if they are using words improperly, and it is my job to help you understand if you are using words improperly. (y) That's a very dramatic word to use, the words you should use for that expression is; "Oh, darn!"[1] (x) I know you need a word to express how upset you are, but when you use that kind of word it is similar to using a word that would hurt or insult someone. (w) If someone calls you a name, it is better to walk away or tell a teacher/ parent, so we can help you resolve the issue or find a way to tell that person exactly what you mean. (v) If you call someone a name because they took something from you, how do you expect to solve that problem? If you say hurtful things to that person instead of talking about **what** happened then you will have **two** problems to solve. --You can discuss the problem without anyone's feelings getting hurt. It's too much work to solve the problem **and** then have to apologize for hurting their feelings.[2]	Don't use that word, I didn't raise you to speak like that.(z) Mommy doesn't like it when you use those words / bad words. (y) Don't you dare use that language in this house.(x) If you ever use that word again, I'll wash your mouth out with soap. (w) If you say that word one more time, I'll smack you so hard, you won't be able to talk for a week. (v) Do you think it makes me feel good to hear you use language like that? You don't even know what that word means - don't use words you don't know the meaning of. (u) Sweetheart, I'm horrified, where did you pick up language like that / where did you hear that word / which one of your friends did you pick up that language from? --You are never going to go to their house again, that's for sure.[1]

XV COMMUNICATION / LITERACY
DEVELOPMENT / LANGUAGE ARTS

Cognitively-Correct™:	Cognitively-incorrect:
Perhaps I've been unclear about this rule / this activity, let's go over it / work on this together.	I've told you a thousand times not to do that. (z) How many times have I told you...
There are times to take turns and times to play alone, and sometimes times you may want to share a toy or treat with a friend. He's just feeling different than you are today. Some days you'll want to play alone without taking turns, and that'll be okay too. For now we'll find something else for you to do.[3]	Don't pay any attention to him - don't waste your time with friends who are being selfish. (z) Well maybe you'll understand what it feels like now, because you've been selfish with your things sometimes.(y) You see what happens when people are being selfish, that's why I tell you never to be that way. (x) If he doesn't want to share just forget about it and find something else to do, or someone else to play with.[2]
Books are better when they are preserved so you can read them over and over again. Magazines and coloring books are for writing and cutting.	Don't write in your books. (z) Hey, I don't spend my hard-earned money on good books so you can cut them or rip them up.
If you whine while you speak it makes it very difficult to understand what you're saying, take a minute to relax and collect your thoughts so we can spend a little time talking.	Just be quiet and quit your whining. (z) Just keep whining and see what it gets you. (y) I'll be damned if I'm going to listen to you whine all day.

XV COMMUNICATION / LITERACY DEVELOPMENT / LANGUAGE ARTS

Cognitively-Correct™:	Cognitively-incorrect:
Please tell me what you expected to happen when you put your shoes in the bathtub / put your toy in the garbage? –What is it that you really wanted to get done? We'll have to spend some time getting this cleaned up. You'll have to show me that you can take care of your things before we get you something new.	What on earth were you thinking? (z) What is wrong with you? - You can't put your shoes in the bath. (y) Don't expect me to buy you anything new for a long time.
What are you planning to do right now/ at this moment?	Don't even think about it!
That belongs inside the toy chest. (z) Please put that underneath the bed / next to / beside / in back of / in front of, etc.[4]	That doesn't go there / That doesn't belong there. Did I say you could put that just anywhere, put it where it belongs
The correct word is...(z) The word you used means -----(y) Would you like me to write it for you?	It's not --- It's ---(z) Don't use words you don't know the meaning of!
You'll have to explain yourself again (z) Why do you think that makes sense (y) Let's try asking him in a different way.	Why are you talking to him that way, do you really think he's going to share his toys with you when you talk/act like that? - That doesn't make any sense.

XV COMMUNICATION / LITERACY DEVELOPMENT / LANGUAGE ARTS

Cognitively-Correct[tm]:	Cognitively-incorrect:
Please choose another topic of conversation while others are around. (z) Saying things about others that are unkind can be hurtful to their feelings –when we hurt someone's feelings, it's similar to having your favorite toy broken. The words you use should be useful or kind to others (y) You can leave your toys and games here, and go to the bathroom to finish that conversation, when you have more pleasant things to talk about or have kind things to say about others, you are welcome to join us again.[5]	Don't talk about others in mean or nasty ways. (z) I don't want to hear you talking like that. Is that the way you want people to talk about you? I don't care who you heard talking that way, I never want to hear you talking like that. It's not okay just because someone else's mom didn't say anything about it.[3]
You have to speak up / speak clearly and ask kindly. Please remember to use good manners, say "please" and "thank you".	I'm not going to listen to you if you mumble and cry like that and you're not getting a thing if you don't say "please".
What do you need? Speak a little louder and ask him these exact words, Can I please play with… (z) Maybe he misunderstood what you said. What did you say exactly? --Try using this phrase – or these words instead --.	Well if you don't make yourself clear, he's not going to read your mind. Go ask him again.
You put that on backwards, take it off and turn it around (z) You have your shoes on the opposite feet, take them off and switch them. We can write your shoes names inside – right and left, or we can give them some other names if you like.	You put that on the wrong way / You've got your shoes on the wrong feet, come here, let me do that for you.

XV COMMUNICATION / LITERACY DEVELOPMENT / LANGUAGE ARTS	
Cognitively-Correct[tm]:	Cognitively-incorrect:
I'm glad you enjoy writing, practice as much as you like.[6]	You've written these numbers the wrong way. (z) You've written those numbers backwards, let me show you how they are supposed to be written. (y) This is the correct way to write those letters/ numbers
You can read the story however you choose. Pictures tell a story as well. I can help you read the words if you like.	You're reading that incorrectly / the wrong way. (z) You're mispronouncing the words, look at all the letters and sound them out correctly. (y) It doesn't matter if it's difficult, you think everything I have to do is easy!? (x) It doesn't matter if you don't like reading, you'll have to read all your life, so you may as well get started early. (w) You can't get into the advanced place Kindergarten if you don't know how to read.
You should have a variety of play activities, and that includes some quiet playtime. Please sit down and do some drawing or reading.	You can't play all the time. You have to practice your reading and writing. (z) You're not going to spend the rest of your life playing, you have to learn to read and write too.

The Content of this section reflects the diverse nature of communication and literary skills compared with other functional developments.

COMMENTS AS QUESTIONS:

GENERAL LANGUAGE ARTS QUESTIONS

- I'd like to see you use your coloring books or old magazines for cutting and drawing. Can we agree on that?
- Do you really think that's the best thing to do with good books?
- If you need more writing materials, you know you can ask me, right?
- Do you have something kind or complimentary to say about that person?
- Do you know that it's difficult to understand what you are saying when you are whining and crying?
- Can you please speak up?
- Do you remember what words to use when you are asking for something?
- Did you try asking again / Did you try asking a second time?
- Will you please tell me why you thought that was the best way to take care of that?
- I'd like you to consider spending the remainder of your playtime doing something different, could you find something else to do?

THE HOW AND WHY OF COGNITIVELY CORRECT

1. If your Child is very verbally expressive, they are probably going to use something, so give them something more appropriate to use.
2. One of parent's worst horrors is to hear their children using inappropriate language [or to witness their Child hitting

someone]. It is a strange twist of fate, but if we criticize children about their choice of words or belittle them in order to impress the feelings behind the use of bad words, we ironically reinforce that hurtful words are a justifiable means of communicating. Children learn language from their parents and caretakers, they learn the feelings behind words before they learn the technical meaning of words, and children are more emotional than technical or intellectual. It is our job to teach them what to say, how to speak and how to use language effectively. If you react emotionally to words children use, you give them the power to control your mood and give them the message that wrong or bad words have more power than good or right words. Children are unable to classify qualities of attention - they want it and need it – which ever kind you want to give, they want to have! You're better off pretending that they've intended to say or do something worthy or "good" and redirect children according to the good intentions you propose and assume for them. Humorously or calmly give them words that express what they mean to say, or ask them questions about something they mean to describe, get a kid's dictionary, look up new words, laugh and have some fun with communication.

3. It's only natural to feel uneasy when your Child is either on the giving or receiving end of a selfish tactic and most parents worry that they'll fail to raise a selfless Child. But jumping the gun and forcing them to share is counteractive in developing an ability to feel charitable or benevolent, because it is necessary to feel that you own possessions in order to give them. Making a decision to give has to be backed by the freedom to own, possess and be responsible for possessions. Children need to experience the freedom of unconditional

receiving before they learn anything. If whatever children own is contingent upon someone else's conditions for usage – where's the incentive to give if the incentive to receive and own has a mixed message. The first step towards learning to share is by first learning to take turns without the judgment or guilt for deciding otherwise. Selfishness is cultivated from a whole cross section of unrefined qualities and poorly nurtured needs. Although the intention is good, forcing children to share will probably do more damage than good.

4. Intricate parts of language are still in the discovery stage for Preschoolers, use them with specific demonstrations – play a game.

5. The urge to dictate may feel like a parental right, but children need to feel and learn that they own their thoughts and words as much as their feelings. Children's naturally good motives have to be fostered and given attention. If children are made to believe that anyone else is the dictator of their thoughts and feelings – who and what will they follow when they're older? Freedom of speech is a right for all humans, let children know there are social effects – tolerances and intolerances.

6. Writing for children before the age of five, is still about creativity, discovery, experimentation, small motor control, developing a purpose for literacy and writing, fueling their personal desire for writing, and the freedom for doing things on their own and in their own way. If you insist on their getting it right before they can freely indulge in the these prerequisites, this "subject" can become a burden, when it's supposed to be fun. Although a few children are exceptions to these rules, and unless you have a crystal ball, let them enjoy doing it in whatever forms they manifest them. Remember it is children's primary "job" to play.

THE HOW AND WHY OF COGNITIVELY INCORRECT

1.   Exploration and discovery cover the same strides in the Language Arts, Communication and Literacy functions as other areas of development. Preschool children are still learning the influences of communication in their interactive experiences. It's preferable to teach children how to adjust their use of words rather than stifle their ability to be, or feel expressive. Language everywhere is full of negative impressions that seem overwhelming. But children are mostly impressed by the guidance they receive from their parents. You can make a difference in children's learning processes when you guide them with positive, creative options that appeal to their learning inclinations and their insatiable compulsions to discover, explore and interact with the people they love most – their family members.

2.   Take a minute or two to observe the age-appropriate toys for Preschool children and you will realize that it is impossible to share them and the only logical process is to take turns. Still, even Preschool children should be introduced to the concept of sharing, and there is nothing wrong or unusual for them to do so, but should do so of their own volition. In terms of Language Arts development, the idea here is to create distinctions between different terms and phrases, but without the negative criticism about your or any other Child's processes of discovery and exploration. Children can take turns with toys, or they can share a banana split.

3.   You can only regulate your own Child's manners and social etiquette.

USEFUL MATERIALS/SUPPLIES

✓ Books
✓ Access to writing materials
✓ Mini-carrying notebook
✓ Central writing pad (to be posted on family fridge)
✓ Journal (for dictation of children's experiences, feelings, thoughts, events, creative stories, etc.)
✓ Common items for discussion and literacy purpose development;
✓ food labels,
✓ signs,
✓ ads/billboards,
✓ name labels,
✓ clothes tags,
✓ photos.
✓ Early Childhood card games.
✓ Creative uses with a tape recorder;
✓ Record children playing,
✓ repeating phrases of a storybook,
✓ conversations, dictation of verbally created stories and conversations.
✓ Chart listing favorite expressions, and respectful phrases.

APPENDIX B:

*Competition is mentally and emotionally an abstract and complicated concept. It is cognitively unbalanced because feelings weigh more than thoughts in Preschool development and competition requires more sophisticated planning and thought processes.

Comparison – a fundamental cognitive/math skill, is a component, a link in a chain of other math concepts/skills, such as patterns, sequencing, classification, sorting, matching, etc., that are still in the development stages. Ultimately – later on – when children will have acquired an ability to substantially connect and use these abilities, they'll have a provision for hypothesizing which supports the ability for executing complicated processes such as competition. Realistically, however, competition is unnecessary in any stages of development, because refining personal abilities means doing the best possible according to individual potential.

During preschool development, since the totality of these skills are still in a state of acquisitions and mergers, asking a preschool Child to compete among their peers would be similar to asking a baby to speak articulately just because they can hear and make sounds. Often children say things that we interpret as competition such as bragging to others that they have finished first with this or that they are better than anyone in that.

When young children accomplish something, it is **relative** and important to them. Requesting certain premeditation for competition among others is too abstract when they are still learning to discover separate characteristics of themselves, let alone merge them for a single purpose or in comparison to anyone else. Mentally seizing or foreseeing an actual effect is extremely difficult for them to grasp or envision. (Thus, you have, "It's *not* fair", "Are we there yet"?). Something that is prominently and concretely displayed before their own eyes is what qualifies their ability to compare for now, thereby realizing what they have, or what they are lacking. Advanced math or abstract concepts, especially 'theories of relativity' are achieved with intellectual and emotional maturity.

Once the stage of preschool intellectual foundations have been developed through diversified interlaced activities, and based on normal emotional development, only then can a combination of these separate functions be integrated in a fashion that inspires improvement through competition, provided it is done in a healthy manner, and certainly beyond the preschool stage of development.

Proposing, enforcing or encouraging preschool children's behavior or potentials by comparing their abilities to others is damaging to their personal esteem before they fully realize they have one.

You have to constantly make deposits in your Child's emotional bank account by trusting and believing in them and **their** accomplishments without having them 'incur' a 'debt' against themselves that requires them to mortgage your expectations without the collateral of a particular ability. They should be able to bear interest in their own personal achievement account, and they should **own** their 'earnings' without 'borrowing' from someone else, just to keep up with the Joneses. Personal wealth is accomplished by saving and reinvesting. The deposits you make in your Child's account are your genuine investments in them. If you are going to borrow or use credit for your investment in them - by making them mirror someone else's abilities - one of you or both of you are going to pay back dearly.

When it comes to praising or reprimanding your own children, you can only make withdrawals if you have made deposits in **their** account. If they are bearing interest based on your secured-deposits, you can fully credit them for what they do, because it has been done with your genuine investment and interest in them.

If you think it's fair to compare your Child with others, then you must fairly relinquish any judgments toward them for engaging in activities "just because others are doing it" – whether they are right or wrong, good or bad. If you teach them to compare, what right do you have to complain when they compare themselves alongside peers or fall into peer pressure when they are older?

It's better to feel that we approve of our own competent abilities rather than feel pressured to *gain* approval from others.

Competition is fine in the later years of development and at that point you can draw on the interest of a shared account that has been fully vested with your genuine encouragement and love that help children endure the discipline needed to develop their potentials.

In simple terms, your Child has to know that their own individual progress is important to you, in comparison to themselves.

Consider children's ability to use computers with such expertise. Why are they so good? It's a few different reasons that really equal one total reason. When preschool children are **free** to play, discover and explore, they easily acquire intuitive attributes in activities of consistent interest and involvement. So, if they do that with computers, they can do that with other skills? –We can make them experts in anything by the time they are 12 years old – right?! Wrong! One of the main reasons they can do what they do with computers is because they are free from the judgments and comparisons we would make about their ever-refining skills. Overall we know less about computers than they do. While they are free from judgments or criticisms to do things this way or that way - according to adult's expectations - they are free to explore, discover and imagine – developing intuitive skills that require the *lack* of mundane instructions and protocol.

Unfortunately with other skills we hover over them with the expectations that they must adopt adult's methods for doing things, and forget that children are still at the mercy of their parents for emotional security and maturity, so children adjust …. In addition to that, using computers is just one skill and total intellectual development requires the use of many skills that are set on emotional capabilities containing the motives for children to use constant, new, acquiring intellectual information.

Children must be in a position to be children, act like children and play like children. If we treat them or expect them to perform as adults, to be like adults, and to make comparisons as adults do, then they'll begin acting as adults, which is beyond their emotional-cognitive abilities however 'smart' they may be.

Children have a right to own their own feelings and thoughts, but that should never mean they are in a position to tell parents what to do or what is best. Their feelings, rights, opinions, personal abilities and social skills are subject to good and firm guidance from parents.

Here's a theory to contemplate: Baby Boomers were raised by parents whose parents managed to survive world wars and economic depression. They literally had nothing and were probably shamed into believing –by their own parents - that their survival was enough to be grateful and happy about. They probably raised their own children (the Baby-Boomers) under the constant critique and guilt that, as war generation children, they had nothing to play with and only one item of clothing to wear. They gave their children more than they had, however little that may have still been, but probably imparted a heaping dose of guilt for having as much. It started the golden age of comparing, labeling and incessant guilt.

The qualifications and requisites for understanding how to create a Childhood for your children, comes from having had the opportunity of being a Child yourself. If the responsibility of Childhood –which is to enjoy the freedom of playing – is replaced by anything other than that freedom and requisite, it confuses the roles and positions of who is entitled to what, and who is responsible for whatever. When role positions are denied or confused, blame steps in to account for who should do this or that and who is responsible for that or this.

Many parents today are afraid to be parents because being a parent means subjecting children to the pain and shame they experienced in their own Childhoods. We've been happier as adults, so it will suffice to treat our children as adults and introduce them to all the wonders of adult life.

Displaced responsibility now comes in all versions – children tell parents what to do, parents tell teachers what to do and children, more than ever, are made to feel entirely responsible for the issues and problems they incur for the lack of Childhood freedom and development.

Meanwhile, many parents, adults and educators claim that while they were kids, they never had the problems that kids have today. But we have had them, we're carriers of them and they were only deferred until we became adults and now they are being poured directly into the souls of children today.

What is the difference between then and now? We have championed children's rights, and rightly so. But we still have a way to go before we fully understand children's developing rights that, in turn, effect living as fully-bloomed-potential-fulfilling adults.

We may feel that we have created some chaos by opening the floodgates of children's freedom and rights. Nevertheless, while we are in the midst of figuring out how to constitutionalize rights according to respective positions and responsibilities, the flow for demanding rights has given us an opportunity that we have probably never seen before in all of history– children feel freer earlier in their lives about acting out the pain and fears of their challenges, whereas earlier generations were pressured into suppressing feelings under the motto of; "Children should be seen and never heard".

That is a major advantage when you consider that problems are better remedied in the developmental years than in the adult years. If we are tackling problems and challenges earlier in people's lives, it may mean that we are getting closer to preventing the struggles that limit people's lifestyles when they are older and have grown out of the developmental stages.

Children should learn based on their abilities, but does that mean they should be exempt from learning certain subjects? Hardly! All the interconnected processes and principles of the world that are worth learning about, and indeed should be learned – especially math and science followed by literature and world history that have shaped our cultures and languages, together give us a firm understanding of who we are. When we acquire a firm understanding of our nature and background, we can create firm guidance that is plausible enough to support all of our capabilities and natural human aptitudes. Anything we learn is going to require less effort when we feel an affinity or connection with it. We can develop a love of learning these subjects when they are introduced in the Preschool years of development through diversification, free-play, discovery and exploration in open-ended activities.

XVI

CREATIVITY

XVI CREATIVITY	
Cognitively-Correct[tm]:	**Cognitively-incorrect:**
Would you like to tell me something about your drawing?[1]	That's a beautiful drawing, what is it?[1]
We have tools and equipment to do that kind of activity, please keep your reading books in good condition.	You can't just cut up whatever you want. (z) Do you think you deserve to have new books if you cut them up and treat them like that?
That's a very colorful and creative way to put a hole in a paper.	Stop drawing over the same spot, you're going to put a hole in the paper, and it'll be ruined.
Before you get started, we'll put a plastic cover on the table / floor / rug.	If you don't put something underneath your drawing paper, you'll ruin the table.
We only do messy play in the kitchen /terrace bathroom / backyard. Please clean up and then we'll move your project/ activity to the kitchen / terrace, etc.	No, you can't spread putty and clay all over the rug and play with it. If we have to end up throwing this rug away, you are going to get the biggest time out of your life.

XVI CREATIVITY

Cognitively-Correct[tm]:	Cognitively-incorrect:
We only cut paper, if you misuse the scissors again, I will take them away for the rest of the day, you will have another chance tomorrow to use them.	If you cut any holes in my good couch, I promise you'll never see another pair of scissors as long as you live.
You'll have to get started cleaning these walls right now, and I'll be removing your crayons for a couple of days. You will still have a chance to do some writing with chalk outside on the driveway / sidewalk.	What do you think you're doing, that's never going to come out? If we have to pay for these walls to be painted, you won't be getting any birthday presents, so you'd better think twice.
You are entitled to use your toys the way you choose. If you use them to damage things or hurt anyone, you will lose your privilege /We'll have to put this away for a while.	How could you be so careless? Do you thing I buy you good toys so that you can destroy things or hurt others?
We have to stay seated while we do cutting, drawing and painting activities. (z)Please put the scissors/paint down before you get up and walk around. If you get up again with the scissors in your hand, we'll put your supplies away immediately, and you'll have to do something else for a while. If you really want to do that much moving around, perhaps you should go outside and run around for a little while.[2]	You can't run around the house with a paintbrush or pair of scissors in your hand. (z) If you fall down and poke your eyes out with those scissors, you'll be sorry. (y) That's right, when you lose an eye or cut your face, maybe then you'll appreciate what you have. (x) Why can't you just go outside and play?

XVI CREATIVITY	
Cognitively-Correct™:	**Cognitively-incorrect:**
You can have a Mommy-lipstick when you're older, if you'd like, I can get you a children's- lipbalm.	No, you can't have my lipstick, I pay good money for these / You're too young for lipstick, don't ask again, nice girls don't wear lipstick.
Please use only the tape you need. If you want to play with the tape, please take only two or three pieces, and then put the dispenser away. (z) Please only use the tape on cardboard or paper, keep it away from the furniture and walls.	Don't play with the tape. (z) Don't waste the tape. (y) Don't put tape all over the walls and furniture, you'll ruin them.
You still have to ask permission to touch my belongings. Please put away the things you were playing with and when you're done, I'll let you choose one pair of my shoes, and one dress and handbag to play with / pair of your father's shoes, tie, old wallet.	You can't just take my things without asking / What makes you think you can just help yourself to my things, you can't play with my good clothes / Don't ever go in my closet again, you've got your own things to play with, leave my stuff alone.
We'll find or purchase some old clothes for you to play with, this way you can play with them whenever you want. I understand it's difficult to remember or ask permission all the time. You either have to ask permission to use other people's things or you can choose your own anytime you want / I'll dig up some old mommy and daddy clothes for your personal play use.	My closet isn't a boutique, you can't just go in there and use things without asking me. I don't want anyone messing around with my personal things, they're not yours, they're mine.[2]

XVI CREATIVITY	
Cognitively-Correct™:	**Cognitively-incorrect:**
Keep your crayons and pencils in their respective cases.	Don't leave your crayons lying around everywhere.
You can draw whenever you feel like doing so. (z) As soon as dinner is finished, you are free to continue drawing.	Don't draw now / Now is not a good time. (z) You can't draw during dinnertime.
Pencils and crayons break, there's nothing wrong with that, they'll just be shorter and last less time.	Don't press so hard on your crayons / That's what happens when you don't take care of your things, before you know it, they'll be gone.
The colored pencils can only be used for drawing, because they have a point on the end. Never point sharp items at others.	Don't wave those pencils around, are you trying to stab someone or poke their eye out?
Place your wet painting gently on the counter. Use both hands to carry it please.	Don't drag/throw your wet painting around / on the floor.
If you'd like something gooey to play with, I have a surprise for you in the kitchen. My make-up has to remain clean and stay packed away in the cosmetic case.--You can play with some whipped cream on the kitchen counter / shaving cream on a table-mat / in the bathtub.	How dare you play with my expensive make-up. I'm very disappointed in you, you know that I don't want you in my cosmetic bag. Go play with your own stuff, you have plenty of your own things.
If you want to do something really messy, you can put on your messy play clothes and do some finger-painting in the bathtub / Play outside.	You can't paint now, I just cleaned the whole house, you'll make a mess of everything (z) I don't want you to make any messes right now.

XVI CREATIVITY	
Cognitively-Correct™:	**Cognitively-incorrect:**
Please save the paper you scribbled on instead of throwing it away / put it in the recycling bin. That paper can be used for cutting or to make collages.	Don't waste paper. Paper costs money. If you don't take care of your things, I'll take them away / be nice to your things.
If you press very gently with the felt-tip pens, the ink will last a longer time.	Don't press so hard. I won't be running out to buy new ones when the ink's all gone.
We'll have to put more newspaper around your painting area / go outside to paint.	Don't make such a mess while you're painting. (z) You're getting paint on my good furniture.
When we get back home, you can do some more painting. Take some paper and colored pencils / crayons with you. You can draw in the car on the way to the supermarket / on our trip.	You can't paint now, we're leaving in five minutes / Now's not the time to start painting.
You must really be enjoying yourself, let me know when you are finished so I can give you some clean-up supplies.	Don't make such a mess, or we'll just put everything away.
This is the area that we do messy play. Please stay in this area to do this activity. When you're done you can do your 'messy-play-cleaning-activity' in this same area.	Don't go anywhere else in the house with that. It's too messy, I just cleaned the house, I'm not going to clean it again. Find something else to do.

XVI CREATIVITY

Cognitively-Correct™:	Cognitively-incorrect:
When you're done playing with something, that's when it should be put away / You have too many things out at once. Let's stop for a minute and choose 2 or 3 things that you'd like to use and put the rest away until 'later'.[3]	You can't take all of your toys out at the same time and make this big mess/ leave them all over the place. This place looks a tornado hit it, you've got to clean it up. (z) If you don't put some of this stuff away right now, you'll be up all night cleaning this mess. (y) This is not the way I expect you to take care of your things, if you don't clean this mess right now, I'm going to pack it all away in boxes and give it to some underprivileged children somewhere. (x) *I need* you to show me that you appreciate having all these things by taking care of them, clean up right now.
If you are enjoying being creative with your face and want to make faces, I'll let you borrow my compact mirror/go to the dressing table mirror, and make all the faces you like, so you can see what you look like.	Nice children don't make faces like that. (z) Stop making faces at people. (y) Stop making ugly faces, one day you'll wake up and your face will look like that forever.
Are you sticking your tongue out because you're hungry or thirsty? / Tongues are for tasting and talking or making faces to yourself in the mirror.	Don't stick your tongue out like that. (z) That's nasty, if you stick your tongue out like that again, I'll smack you / it will fall off.

XVI CREATIVITY

Cognitively-Correct[tm]:	Cognitively-incorrect:
Dinner is for eating, clay and putty is for sculpting. Please *eat* your dinner, so that you can have your dessert. When you're done, you can play with some clay or putty and make a sculpture –and if you like, we'll take photos of it.[4]	Don't make sculptures with your food (z) Don't play with your food, or you'll go to bed without any dinner, don't you know there are hungry children in this world?[3]
When you're older, I'll buy you a porcelain doll as a collector's item. Right now, you need dolls that you can handle and play with. Porcelain dolls can shatter and break, and then you'd have to just throw them away. (z) Porcelain dolls are just for looking at. They are display items, or collector's items. Perhaps we could buy one to decorate your room, but if falls and it breaks apart, you will lose your decoration.[5]	I bought some pretty porcelain dolls to decorate your room, but you can't touch them or play with them, because they're very expensive and they can break, they are meant only as a decoration.[4]
Please put your dress shoes away and put your play shoes back on. If you want to play dress-up, then you can borrow a pair of my shoes (z) take out your adult-play clothes. (y) If you want fancy shoes, we can decorate your play shoes with some ribbons, or we'll tape some pretty tissue/wrapping paper on your shoes.	You can't wear your dress shoes to play, you'll ruin them. Do you think I'm just going to run out and buy you new dress shoes whenever you scuff them, I'm not made of money![5]

XVI CREATIVITY	
Cognitively-Correct™:	*Cognitively-incorrect:*
If you want to play with food or liquid, I'll fill a large pot/basin with dry noodles and dry rice, you can keep it in your play area to use whenever you wish. I have some extra plastic cups and wooden spoons and a funnel for you to keep as part of that activity. I'll even let you have your own dust-pan and broom to *gather* the extra/loose rice and noodles that escape from the basin. We can 'color' the noodles and rice too.*	You can't play in the kitchen sink while I'm cooking dinner. (z) Find something else to do, water isn't the only thing to play with.[6]

COMMENTS AS QUESTIONS

COMMON CREATIVE ACTIVITIES

- Are we allowed to cut anything other than paper or cardboard?
- What are you going to use your scissors for?
- Have we forgotten something? – What do we put on the table before any messy play activities?
- Are you going to miss that toy if it breaks?
- Are those your scissors or my scissors you're using?
- Do we use scissors while we're standing or sitting?
- What are the only materials we put tape on?
- Where do we put the wet paintings when we're finished?
- What do we do with the colored pencils and crayons when we're finished using them?

- Do you want to do your messy play activity inside – in the messy play area – or would you rather go outside where there's more space?
- Which toys are you playing with right now?
- Do you know how much time we designate for cleaning the messy play area before our next activity/before dinnertime?
- Do you understand that we only play with food if it's part of our play activity area/supplies?
- What do we do with mealtime food?

INNOVATIVE/CREATIVE LEARNING ELEMENTS & TOOLS

- Do you realize that if you use that differently than it's real use that it may break or be ruined?
- Would you like to do something new?
- How do we handle delicate items?
- Can you handle this gently, with care?
- How do we handle things that can break?
- Do you want to do some drawing in the car on our way to...?
- Do we play or eat together at dinnertime?
- You can stay here with us without making faces while we have company or you can go stand in front of your bedroom/bathroom mirror to make faces, which do you prefer?
- What kind of shoes do we wear while we're playing?

THE HOW AND WHY OF COGNITIVELY CORRECT

1. Drawing is a process! It's very important for the Child to talk about what he/she was thinking about when they created this drawing.

2. If you say "once more", be firm and gentle, stick to the mandate, and help your Child make a transition to another activity. It is unnecessary to be critical or ulcerate the situation with a lecture. Action will convey what you mean.

3. They may have a contrary opinion about 'too many' and believe they have set up quite the play zone. Indulge their opinion, and stick to an aspect of the issue. Tell them they must choose 2 or 3 items to play with and the rest should be put away because all the walking space is covered. If they stall, start putting things away starting with the main interest toy, they'll make objections, you can apologize explaining that it is better done by them, since they know what's most important.

4. You accept their artistic capabilities, but you expect them to eat! – only a handful of children will do this consistently, because their hands need to be in constant creative motion. Just give them plenty of other outlets to fulfill their sculpting inclinations.

5. Children want to touch everything. New and beautiful things are always a temptation. Anything breakable is better omitted from children's personal living space or décor.

THE HOW AND WHY OF COGNITIVELY INCORRECT

1. You're cutting off one of the best opportunities to converse with your Child and to find out what their thoughts and interests or struggles might be.

2. This is an ideal time to remember that most things children do are basically and simply impulses of discovery and exploration. Some of those include imitating others, and bonding rituals, such as wearing parents clothing. You have to decide what limits you want to make.

3. It's all meant well, but everyone's appetite wanes and peaks.

Awareness and appreciation will be better served if you 'involve' them in feeding the hungry – let them drop the donation check in the mailbox, tag along to drop food and warm coats at local soup kitchen, etc. But – making them feel guilty will fail to make an impression.

4. Who wanted the dolls? If you purchase something that is for your Child on your terms, then you confuse the lines of ownership and entitlement. Let the Child be the Child and play with the dolls on her terms or take them away put them in your room.

5. Preschoolers are steadfast once they're involved in something, but in certain situations you can make modifications that will suit you both.

6. Keep in mind that children often need guidance or direction in finding *other* things to do.

USEFUL MATERIALS / SUPPLIES CHECKLIST

- ✓ Finger paint
- ✓ Pencils/colored pencils
- ✓ Children's scissors
- ✓ Sand
- ✓ Water
- ✓ Beans, rice, noodles*
- ✓ Stickers glue/colored, sparkled
- ✓ Paper, colored/construction paper, magazines, newspaper
- ✓ Coloring books
- ✓ Old clothes and shoes
- ✓ Shovels, pails, old wooden spoons and utensils
- ✓ Plastic containers
- ✓ Old spray bottles
- ✓ Paper plates
- ✓ Puppets

✓   Listening and dance music

*Spread newspaper on the counter. In a plastic bowl, pour
a cup of dry rice and/or noodles. Add a few drops of food
coloring to 2 tablespoons of isopropyl alcohol. Pour into
bowl of noodles and rice and stir with a spoon until the
color has covered all of the noodles / rice. Vary/make
batches with different colors. Lay out the noodles and/or
rice spaciously on the newspaper to allow alcohol to dissi-
pate overnight. Mix the variety together in the large basin.
Enjoy, play together.

✓   Short pieces of yarn (no longer than 3/4 inches)
✓   Ribbons (same length, unless you help them cut if for a specific
    purpose)
✓   Tape, Children's liquid or glue sticks
✓   Shaving cream (supervised)
✓   Cool whip
✓   Jello
✓   Pipe cleaners
✓   Playing putty, or clay
✓   General materials to make collages or pinatas
✓   Bubbles and wands (Homemade bubbles can be made with
    dish-washing liquid and some corn syrup and water. Bubble
    wands can be made with pipe cleaners. Large bubble wands
    for use outside so that children can run with it; tie a plastic
    hanger to a branch or similar stick. Make solution in open,
    wide, flat basin or bucket to dip hanger-bubble-wand).

XVII

SELF

XVII SELF	
Cognitively-Correct[tm]*:*	*Cognitively-incorrect:*
Are you upset, come here, let's sit down and talk about it. (z) I'm sorry you're upset about this. (y) Do you need a hug? (x) Can I offer you a tissue?	Don't cry! (z) Stop crying (y) Come here, I'll give you something to cry about (x) What are you crying for?
You seem to be more upset than usual about this sort of thing, could you please tell me if there's something else bothering you? (z) Are you hungry, tired? Do you miss Daddy / Grandma – would you like to give him/her a call? (y) Do you need to get some fresh air, should we take a little walk? (x) You're allowed to be upset and cry about whatever you want, if crying makes you feel better, everyone feels that way sometimes. (w) If it means that much to you, we'll change your candy day, movie day, play date, etc. Let's make a note of it on the calendar.	That's nothing to cry about. (z) I don't want to hear you crying about it. (y) Crying is not going to change anything. (x) Don't cry and have a tantrum just cause you can't have your own way. (w) Crying is not going to get you anything.

XVII SELF	
Cognitively-Correct[tm]:	*Cognitively-incorrect:*
I understand your disappointment , but it's dangerous to go swimming when there's a lightening and thunderstorm, we'll have to choose another activity for you to do today.	We can't go in the pool today, that's all there is to it, so don't cry about it, if you're going to cry, you can go to your room.
Please mind your manners, when we get home you can act as silly as you like.	You can't act that way when we go out, stop being so ridiculous.
While we're out we have to show our best manners wherever we go. First we're going to the library, and after we'll go to the park. Let's go over our manners and the rules we follow in public; Remember to whisper in the library, we have to choose a book quietly, and if someone is in your way please say "excuse me". Let's display the same manners as we do in our favorite places. If you're having trouble remembering the rules, I'll remind you, but if too many reminders cause a disturbance, we'll have to come home right away.	Be good and mind your manners, if you don't behave, we'll go home and you'll get a time-out / If you don't stop doing that, you won't have a treat. (z) We won't go to the park later. (y) I'll take away one of your privileges.
If you continue to act this way (run off, yell inside library, taking kid siblings toys, accidentally kicking things, throwing things around, etc.) we'll have to go straight home, you can yell and run around in the backyard / outside.	Be nice, since when do we act like this? (z) If you keep acting like this, we won't go anywhere, you'll just go home and you can forget about going to the park.

XVII SELF	
Cognitively-Correct™:	**Cognitively-incorrect:**
Treats are for sharing, toys are for taking turns. (z) Try asking if your friend is willing to take turns. (y) you can ask if they'll let you take turns. (x) Let's get a timer and everyone can have a turn for ten minutes. (w) Try taking turns, if it causes a lot of commotion we'll put it away for a little while. (v) There's nothing wrong with keeping your personal things to yourself, but it's better to wait until you're alone, then you can play without taking turns. (u) Ask if you can make a trade for this toy.	Hey kids, you have to share, if you don't share then you'll all get a time out and nobody will have anything to play with. (z) You have to share, it's not nice to be selfish.
Please be gentle. (z) Please treat others with the kindness that you'd like from them.	Be nice. (z) That wasn't a nice thing to do.
It's very kind of you to let the baby play with your teddy bear. (z) It was very considerate of you to keep your friend company while he was feeling sad.	That was a nice thing to do.[1]
Please decide whether you want to stay in the shopping cart or get out and help me push, it's one or the other.	You can't keep getting in and out of the shopping cart.
We use words to say how we're feeling or what's bothering us, if you want her to know how you feel you're going to have to choose words that express yourself. Hands are for playing and making things, we never use them to hurt others.	Don't hit. (z) Why did you hit him /her? How would you like to be hit? (y) Don't ever hit anyone.

XVII SELF

Cognitively-Correct[tm]:	Cognitively-incorrect:
If something is bothering you please tell me, there's never any need to say unkind things to others. Let's talk about how you're feeling so I can help you find the words. If it happens again we'll have a time-out again to talk about it.	If you don't have anything nice to say, please don't say anything at all (z) That wasn't a nice thing to say.
Please put the dish down carefully. (z) If you like you can help me crack open the eggs for this afternoon's cookie making activity. (y) You can help me crush the boxes for the recycling.	No, don't do that, be careful. (z) Don't be clumsy . (y) If you don't watch what you're doing, you'll break it. (x) How could you do that? If you're going to help me, you have to do things right.
Please be polite, say "excuse me" and then wait your turn to speak, it'll just take one minute for me to finish my sentence.[1]	Don't interrupt.(z) Don't be rude. (y) You can't just barge in without excusing yourself. (x) Is that any way for a young lady to behave?
Please speak in a quiet tone of voice. Yelling makes it difficult to understand what you are saying.	Be quiet and calm down. (z) Calm down and quit yelling.
Let's do something to calm down a little, and we'll talk about it, do you want to cuddle for a little while or just be on your own?[2]	You just calm yourself down right now. (z) I'm not listening to you until you calm down.[3]
If you want to scream and yell while you play then please play outside. Inside we use quiet voices.	Don't scream!

XVII SELF	
Cognitively-Correct[tm]:	**Cognitively-incorrect:**
Would you like to wear this outfit or that outfit, do you want to dress yourself or would you like some help?	Put this on. (z) Let me dress you. (y) Wear this today.
Please stop and start over again ~ the zipper has to be in the front.[3]	You're doing that the wrong way. (z) You're not doing that right. (y) Let me do it for you.
Of course you can pour your own milk / juice, I'll get a small cup or pitcher for you.	You can't pour your own milk or juice, you'll spill it and get it everywhere.
What exactly are you planning. (z) What do you have in mind?	Don't even think about it.
Do you know where that belongs? (z) Please put it back, can you show me where you found it? (y) We have plenty of candy at home / toys to play with. (x) Would you like to put it back by yourself or would you like me to put it back for you – do you need help?	Put that back. (z) I'm so tired of telling you not to touch things. (y) I didn't say anything about buying that. (x) No, I'm not getting that, you can't have it, and that's that. (w) I don't want to hear anything about it anymore. (v) One more sound from you and you won't get a thing.
You can help me roll all the yarn into a ball if you want to help. I'd like to crochet this sweater on my own, you can have some of your own yarn to make something with, but you have to sit beside me to do this activity. If you decide to do something else, this has to stay here and you can come back to it later.	No, this isn't yours, it's my yarn and I want to do this by myself. (z) It has to be done the right way, you can't help me, it's not for kids.[4]

XVII SELF	
Cognitively-Correct[tm]:	Cognitively-incorrect:
She's still learning to socialize with new faces / friends / friends of family / social circle.(z) She'll get to know you soon enough.[4]	She's shy / He's shy (z) Don't act that way, that's not nice, you can say hello, don't be shy.
I feel there may be something bothering you, because you are acting differently. Are you trying something new or do you feel uncomfortable with something. (z) Did something happen that you'd like to tell me about?[5]	Stop acting like a brat / a cry baby. Why can't you be nice? Stop being a nuisance.(z) What's wrong with you today?
You have to use words to tell me what's bothering you. What you're feeling. (z) It is totally unacceptable to use our hands to hit or hurt anyone.[6]	Mommy doesn't like it when you don't cooperate. (z) Don't hit Mommy. (y) If you hit Mommy again, you're going to get a spanking.[5]
I understand you are upset about leaving and you are free to tell me so / let me know. But our day /our time involves doing many things – this is just one of them. We have other things to do and we'll have other chances to come back here.	I don't want you getting upset every time we leave / about having to leave (z) Every time we leave the park you put up this annoying fuss, I don't like it, I want it to stop.
You have to choose a sport shoe or running shoe for playing and gym activities. You'll have a chance to wear your dress shoes soon / this weekend.	You can't wear your dress shoes to the gym / park, go take them off right now, and put your sneakers on.

COMMENTS AS QUESTIONS

FEELINGS

- Would you like to talk about it?
- What would make you feel better right now?
- Do you want to stay here in the park or go home?
- Do you really believe everything you're saying? Did someone do something to bother you or hurt your feelings that you would say something like that?
- That's the second or third time I've heard you say that about one of your friends, do you think we should consider playing with someone else for a while?
- Do you understand that 'excuse me' means you have something to say, but you still have to wait a couple of seconds while I finish my sentence? I know waiting is difficult.
- What can I do to help you feel calm – please tell me what happened / I see something is upsetting you, please tell me what it is, perhaps we can fix it!?
- We have a messy play date, would you like to wear jeans or sweatpants?
- Do you really think that's the best way to tell me what's going on / what's bothering you?
- Do you really feel that upset about leaving?
- You're entitled to feel the way you want, but you understand that we still have to go now?
- Do you want to talk now or later?

SELF ESTEEM & CONFIDENCE

- Can you tell me what's different today about the way you feel? Did I forget something?
- Would you like to help?
- Do you think you can convince him with words to include you in his play activity, would you like to give it a try? Do we need to sit down and have a talk about how we are going to use our hands?
- Would you like me to pour your milk or would you like to do it yourself?
- Could you try to say hello please / introduce yourself?

SELF IN A GROUP, MORALS, ETHICS, GENERAL

- Do you remember / would you like me to remind you what kind of manners we will have today – or would you rather tell me?
- What kind of voice do we use in the library?
- Can you please try asking if they'll take turns with their toys / belongings.
- Whatever you decide or choose that will be it for the remainder of our time here, do you want to stay in the shopping cart or get out?
- Try again! Could you try a little harder next time?
- Can you please show me where that belongs?
- What's the rule about bringing personal play items to school?
- Do you really think that's the best way to tell me what's going on / what's bothering you?

THE HOW AND WHY OF COGNITIVELY CORRECT

1. Remember to follow through, waiting too long is difficult for young children, the less you schedule children's needs, the more they acquire a disposition for empathy and patience, but this is also an opportunity for them to realize the concept of time provided the time promised is kept.

2. Everyone gets upset for legitimate reasons. Extreme or radical emotion is still a relatively new or even scary experience. Children need support and understanding without judgment or criticism, with a little time and space for processing emotions to get back in control. Causing them to deny or repress how they feel pushes the issue down or away instead of learning how to resolve it. By making it let's or we instead of you, it keeps them from feeling ashamed or singled-out about emotions we all experience.

3. Whatever it is, talk them through it, rather than putting your hand in it. If you do it for them, how will they learn it themselves –Remember, everything is hands-on for preschoolers, the more their hands are involved in a required task, the better they learn to handle it.

4. Avoid label type names or expectations with regards to personality or character. The line of scrimmage here is when do you stop saying it? - When does she start believing it?

5. Remember to offer non-judgmental / non-critical words or phrases to help them identify their thoughts and feelings and also to feel trusted about divulging them.

6. If you want children to use their voices to express themselves, you will have to set the example. Although there schools of thought that favor disciplining with 'light' spanking, it fails to deal with the issue. It may be quelled for the moment

but unreasonable behavior is a clear sign that something is pent-up, and unresolved issues create recurring episodes. Talking resolves – hitting stirs anger which is a combustible.

THE HOW AND WHY OF COGNITIVELY INCORRECT

1. Give specific names to feelings, actions and intentions. "Nice" is used too generally – we need emotional literacy!
2. Monitor and supervise children when handling pets.
3. Being upset is usually a symptom of an issue or event, get to the heart of the issue and the symptoms will subside. Children usually need guidance and help to restore their state of peace. Ask questions without judging or reacting to their reaction.
4. If you allow kids to play with yarn or long string, it must be supervised, but it's always a better idea to give them only pieces of string that are shorter than the length of their hand.
5. Avoid speaking about yourself in the third person, it would be unusual to speak that way with anyone else.

USEFUL MATERIALS / SUPPLIES CHECKLIST

✓ Plaques or signs with children's names
✓ Mirrors
✓ Familiar setting or area for chats
✓ Children's magazines
✓ Special or individual time with one Child
✓ Child size/Child friendly supplies; cutlery, chairs, traditional clock (non-digital), stickers for a sticker chart – fulfilling responsibilities.

Keep in mind that the Child should be separated from an action of wrong doing. Punishment packages the Child with the action.

Paradoxically children may come to think of themselves as that bad action. Giving children an opportunity to take responsibility at that moment offers them a chance to retrace their steps and learn to take control of their actions while they avoid shame.

XVIII

SCIENCE, NATURE
AND THE FIVE SENSES

XVIII SCIENCE, NATURE AND THE FIVE SENSES	
Cognitively-Correct™:	*Cognitively-incorrect:*
We will make plans for a nature and discovery activity. Tomorrow I'll gather some messy play clothes and some clean-up materials. We are wearing dressy clothes today and keeping a neat and clean appearance to have dinner at Grandma's house. For now, please keep your hands clean and stay away from anything messy.	Don't touch anything dirty. (z) Don't pick that up, it's dirty, and full of germs.(y) We're going to Grandmas for dinner so you had better not get a spot of dirt on you. (x) You are not getting dirty today. (w) Can't you guys stay clean for just five minutes, sit down and be still until we go.

XVIII SCIENCE, NATURE AND THE FIVE SENSES

Cognitively-Correct™:	Cognitively-incorrect:
We only put food and drinks in our mouth. The only other things we put in our mouths are the cutlery or straws we use to drink and eat.(z) Our mouths are for eating, drinking, tasting, breathing, talking and smiling, singing and crying. (y) Please keep things away from your mouth that have been on the floor, and never put your mouth or lips on glass or furniture or anything at all.(x) The only thing you can use your lips for are smiling, or whistling, or putting on some chapped lip medicine or to give your loved ones a kiss on the cheek. (w) If you really need to put something in your mouth, then we'll make you a sandwich.	You're not a baby anymore, you know better than to put dirty things in your mouth. (z) Don't put that in your mouth, it has germs all over it. (y) Don't put that in your mouth after it's been on the dirty floor, I don't want you to get sick. (x) Don't put everything you see in your mouth, you're not a garbage can, before I know it, you'll actually start eating the garbage too.
Keep your hands and tongue and mouth away from the icy part of the freezer. If you'd like to taste some ice, we'll take a couple of cubes from the ice tray and put them in a bowl, then you can enjoy them all you like.	Are you crazy, do you want to cut your tongue? Get away from the freezer, it's not for playing.(z)If you hurt yourself there, don't say that I didn't warn you.
We play with dirt outside.(z) The dirt stays outside. (y) Nature has its home outside, plants and dirt can only be inside when they are in a flowerpot.	Don't bring dirt/ mud /leaves/ worms /sticks /rocks - inside the house, I just cleaned everything.

XVIII SCIENCE, NATURE AND THE FIVE SENSES	
Cognitively-Correct[tm]*:*	*Cognitively-incorrect:*
Please keep your hands off the flowers. You can look at them and smell them. (z) If we enjoy their beauty without touching them, they will last for many days.	Don't touch the flowers, they'll just die and then we'll have to throw them away. Just leave the flowers alone.
Please use a tissue to clean your nose.	Don't pick your nose.
Standing in front of the fridge with the door open for a long time is the same as going outside without a coat on during the winter when it's really cold. (z) If you leave the fridge door open for too long then the warm air will go inside, and the food has to stay cold to be preserved.	Do you think I own stock in the electric company or something like that? (z) Just 'cause you don't pay the bill, doesn't mean you can waste energy. (y) Close the fridge door already, you'll catch a cold.
It's better to throw snowballs at trees or walls or fences or a target. (z) If you want to throw snowballs at each other, then please put your swimming goggles on, before getting started and leave them on until you're back in the house. (y) Stay as far away from the house as possible but stay in the yard when throwing snowballs.[1]	Don't throw snowballs, I don't want to hear that a window has broken or that someone is hurt.(z) Throwing snowballs is dangerous, someone can lose an eye, and if you can't think of something fun to do in the snow then you can just come inside.[1]
You can go outside and kick a ball around for a little while, or you can go down to the basement and kick a pillow or a punching bag.	What do you think you're doing, this is not a football stadium you know? (z) Just calm down and find something else to do.

XVIII SCIENCE, NATURE AND THE FIVE SENSES	
Cognitively-Correct[tm]:	Cognitively-incorrect:
You've had two warnings already to stop throwing dirt. Digging in the dirt or looking for small treasures buried beneath the dirt or making mud pies was the activity you agreed to do. Let's wash up and look for something else to do, this activity is over until another day.	I told you not to throw dirt, if I have to warn you one more time, you'll spend the rest of the day in your room. (z) Stop playing with the dirt and don't get dirty, if you drag one bit of dirt into this house, I'll be furious, I'm tired of cleaning up after everyone.
Puddles are lots of fun to splash in, but you must put some waterproof boots on (or put plastic bags over socks - inside of shoes) and a rain-coat, the more your clothes stay dry the longer you can play in the puddles.	Don't splash in the puddles, you'll get all wet. (z) You just can't go around splashing in puddles whenever it rains and wherever we go. (y) It's a lot of work washing those clothes after you get wet; I'm not running a laundry service.
You have to be dressed in a few layers before running through the leaf piles. Sometimes there are fallen branches in the pile that can poke you. and the extra layers can cushion you a bit.[2] (z) Lets collect some leaves for our *Autumn craft activity.	Don't jump in the leaf piles, they're dirty. I just took your clean coats out of the winter storage. (z) I didn't spend hours raking all those leaves so you could make a mess. I worked hard putting those piles together. I'm exhausted as it is.
Screaming or shouting in someone's ear may seem like fun but everyone deserves to have some space. (z) I'm sorry if you feel like she is ignoring you, but it's better to speak with someone face to face if you want to get his or her attention.	Do you want someone to scream in your ear too? (z) What are you trying to do – break their eardrum? (y) Be nice, that's no way to talk to someone.

XVIII SCIENCE, NATURE AND THE FIVE SENSES

Cognitively-Correct™:	Cognitively-incorrect:
Babies can only have baby food in their mouths. Would you like to sit beside me and help feed the baby for a few minutes? Do you want me to take a photo of you and the baby together?	Have you lost your mind, are you trying to choke her to death? Don't put things in the baby's mouth like that. If you're not going to treat her nicely, then I'm not going to let you near her.
When we go to the city zoo, there are signs posted everywhere that say you must keep your hands away from the cages or glass. When we're at the petting zoo, that's where you can touch the animals, that's why it's called a petting zoo. The city zoo animals are only for looking at. The animals there are wild and like to keep their distance from people. If you disrespect the zoo rules, we will have to leave.	Don't bang on the glass/cage. The zookeeper will get mad at you. What if the glass breaks and that animal comes after you, then what will you do? (z) If you do that again, it'll be the last time we ever come back here.
If you really want to tear something apart, I'll get you some cotton wadding or clay. You are free to break them and tear them and cut them in any shapes or forms you please. The other things in the house have to stay intact so we can keep them in good condition. This way they are always available for the purpose we need.	You can't just abuse things every time you get mad about something. I'm going to whip you good if you break anything. (z) Go ahead and kick the table so I can smack you. (y) I will not stand for that kind of behavior, you better straighten up right now or you're going to get the worst punishment of your life.

XVIII SCIENCE, NATURE AND THE FIVE SENSES

Cognitively-Correct™:	Cognitively-incorrect:
If you want the DVD player or VCR player to work all the time without being broken, then you have to be sure to only put DVD's or videos inside of them. If you put small toys or other objects inside the machines, some pieces could be stuck in there. You want it to be here at home where you can use it whenever you want, instead of sitting in the repair shop and miss watching your favorite movies – right!?	You're going to spend the rest of the day in your room for doing that. How could you do something so stupid, don't you know that it could break, you just can't put things inside the video /DVD player?[2]
You have to exercise all parts of your body everyday, including all of your senses. Your eyes and ears need to experience other sounds and sights. If you only watch T.V. or play video games, you'll miss hearing birds sing, or thunder roar, or seeing the sunset, or smelling flowers or finding bugs and smooth stones, chasing squirrels, feeling grass between your fingers, etc. You can give just as much time to doing other things as you can to watching television.	I don't want you to watch television all day. (z) You can't watch the same movie over and over again all day, get out and do something else. (y) If you can't think of something else to do besides just watch T.V. then maybe I should take away all of your videos and disconnect the cable, cause at the rate you're going, you'll turn into a vegetable-head. (x) I'm not going to let you watch television all day, I can't listen to that stuff all day, I'm sick of it.

XVIII SCIENCE, NATURE AND THE FIVE SENSES

Cognitively-Correct™:	Cognitively-incorrect:
Of course we're going to handle and eat the tomatoes once they are finished growing, but in the meantime, they like to be left alone to enjoy the space and air around them. Plants needs and people needs are very different, but plants have feelings too and we should respect them. They need room to grow without feeling disturbed. When they're ripe and it's time to cut them from their branches, you can help me by putting them in a basket, this way you'll have a chance to handle them before they are eaten. (z) Please respect my requests so you can maintain the privilege of helping me in the garden.	I didn't spend all day in the garden just so you could treat it like a playground, why can't you just play nicely somewhere?! Can't I make anything without you tearing into it like some kind of destruction zone? You have plenty of things of your own to take apart, leave my stuff alone. How could you do that after I worked so hard in the garden, does everything I do mean nothing to you? You know how much I love my gardening, how could you do something like that to me?
The clouds sure look like they're made of cotton.(z) Perhaps they're pretending that they're made of cotton candy. They're actually made of fluffy water.	Clouds are not made of cotton, don't be silly. (z) Clouds are not made of cotton candy, whoever told you something stupid like that?
Lots of things look the same but are actually different. Cotton looks very similar to wool, but if you touch them, they feel different, and they may smell a little different too.	They're not the same.(z) Just 'cause things look the same doesn't mean they are the same.

XVIII SCIENCE, NATURE AND THE FIVE SENSES

Cognitively-Correct™:	Cognitively-incorrect:
Cotton wadding and cotton candy look the same and even though they can both have different colors, one is soft and smooth and the other is soft and sticky. Which one do you think tastes better? Which can be eaten?	Cotton candy is not made out of cotton. What makes you say something like that? (z) That's a dumb thing to say, how could they possibly be made out of cotton ?!
Sometimes the moon looks like it is bigger than the sun because it is closer to the earth.[3]	The moon is not bigger than the sun, it just looks that way.
The sun is very hot and very far away, but it's big enough so we can see it and feel its heat.[3]	I don't know a lot about the sun (z) I don't know exactly how far away it is.
Maybe the sky is blue because the sky loves blue, but the sky likes other colors too that's why it changes colors and makes rainbows.[3]	How am I supposed to know that, do I look like an encyclopedia to you?
The sky is friends with the earth, that's why it rains sometimes so it can water the trees and plants and give us water to drink and it washes the dirt out of the sky.[3]	That's just the way it is. I don't know why it has to rain. It has to rain sometimes. There's nothing you can do about it, just deal with it like the rest of us. That's life!
The sun's light shines on the moon, and the reason we only see part of the moon sometimes is because the moon is playing hide and seek with the sun.[3]	The moon doesn't have any light of its own, if there were no sun, then the moon wouldn't shine. The moon changes positions so it doesn't catch all of the sun's light.[3]

XVIII SCIENCE, NATURE AND THE FIVE SENSES

Cognitively-Correct™:	Cognitively-incorrect:
Of course we can make different color pancakes. You'll have to eat them to see if they have different flavors.	What's the point in making different color pancakes, it's just a waste and it's really messy, think of something else to do.
Berries have different colors and shapes and sizes and flavors just like different vegetables. Everything in nature has its own name.	All berries are not the same! Just because you don't like one doesn't mean you'll hate them all. I don't want to hear you saying fruit is 'yucky'.
Ice has to be very cold to keep its shape. You can have an ice cube to play with. Watch what happens when your warm hands keep holding it. Let's see which one melts faster – the one you hold in your hands or the one we leave sitting on the counter.	The water will never turn to ice just cause you keep watching it, and if you don't stop opening the freezer, it'll never be cold enough to turn to ice. Now get out of there before you catch your death of cold, you're wasting electricity. I don't own the electric company.
The water needs about 2 hours before it turns into ice cubes. We can check on it later. Let's have a look at the clock so we can time how long it takes. Let's put an ice cube on the counter to see which takes more time – melting an ice cube or turning water into frozen ice cubes.	It'll be ice when it's ice, why are you bothering me, how am I supposed to know exactly how long it'll take to freeze, I'm not a scientist. When it's frozen I'll let you know. You've got a million toys, can't you find something better to do than worry about the ice in the freezer?

XVIII SCIENCE, NATURE AND THE FIVE SENSES

Cognitively-Correct™:	Cognitively-incorrect:
We can watch the weather channel to see when the snow is expected to stop, or you can watch out the window for a while. Then we'll check the clock to see how long it snowed.	I'm not psychic, I can't tell you when the snow is going to stop for sure. (z) Do I look like the 'weather -person'? Nobody can know everything all the time, give it a rest.
I'm sorry your ball went down the sewer, it's usually impossible to get it out because the sewer is deep or because the rush of the water in the sewer washes it away. Get a larger ball to play with, one that is bigger than the sewer hole. Next time we're out shopping we can look for a ball. I'll put it on our shopping list. But the most important thing is for you to stay away from the sewer or the street. Stay in the yard when you're playing with the ball or wait until we're at the park and away from sewers.	Yeah, well what did you think was going to happen if you threw your ball in the street? Did you think it would magically come rolling back to you and not go down the sewer? Life's tough, do you think you're immune to losing things? It's not worth crying over spilled milk, it's your loss, maybe you'll realize better next time. Do you think I'm just going to run out and buy you something new every time you lose it, what do you think I am – 'Miss Money-bags'?

XVIII SCIENCE, NATURE AND THE FIVE SENSES

Cognitively-Correct™:	Cognitively-incorrect:
Stay away from the garbage, unless you are just throwing something away. It's better to stay away from germs.(z) Are you planning to help me take the garbage out –is that why you're fussing with it? --Let's do it together. (y) Okay, I understand that you lost something in the garbage. Let's take the bag outside and put some rubber gloves on your hands, then you can rummage through the garbage to find whatever you have lost. Once you've found what you're looking for, you can clean up the mess and put every bit of trash back in the bag. If it turns out that it's misplaced somewhere else, it will still be your job to put the trash back, we have to keep things in their natural order when we disturb them. If you still need to look elsewhere for what you've lost, I'll be glad to help you once you're done cleaning up.	That's too bad, you should have thought about it before you threw it in the garbage, you can't just dig around the filthy garbage now for one lousy piece of a toy you should have taken care of. You're not rummaging through the trash now, what's done is done. That's what happens when you don't think. I hope you learned your lesson. Get out of the kitchen, I'm not letting you spread germs everywhere just so you can look for something you should have never thrown away. If you don't learn to take care of your things, you'll lose them. Now it's gone, and I don't want to hear you crying about it either. If you'd just do the things I tell you to do, you wouldn't have to worry about making stupid mistakes.

COMMENTS AS QUESTIONS

EARTH & NATURE ACTIVITIES/ NATURAL ENVIRONMENT

- Do you understand why the garden has to have a fence around it?
- What do you think might happen if you throw the ball really far away?
- What do you think the clouds are made of?
- You understand that fire burns, and that's why we stay far away from the stove while I'm cooking / we never go near the fireplace?
- In what ways do we care for plants – how do we handle them?
- Which types of things are we allowed for use as target practice/ throwing snowballs at? –What is the proper way to dress in cold weather?
- Can you spend some time raking leaves? The rule about running through leaf piles is that we can only do that in our own yard, can you remember that?
- The zoo has rules that we have to follow, can you tell me what you think some of those rules are?
- Why do you think that berries have different shapes and sizes and colors and tastes?
- Why do you think the worm disappeared in the dirt?
- Did you know that the thunder is loud so that everyone can hear it and know that a storm is coming?
- Do you understand why the garden has to have a fence around it?
- What do you think might happen if you throw the ball really far away?

- What do you think the clouds are made of?

FIVE SENSES - INTUITIVE DEVELOPMENT

- What are the only things we're allowed to put in our mouths?
- "Mother Nature" made fish without ears, but they have really good eyesight. Did you know you could get their attention by looking into their eyes?
- Do you think it's necessary to shout in someone's ear – you can hear sounds that are far away that are loud enough, right?
- Can you please repeat the rule about putting things in our mouths? –Do you realize that this rule is to keep our teeth in good condition and keep our mouths healthy and safe?
- Would you like to help me look through a local magazine to find a new touching/hands-on/messy play activity?
- If you only play on the computer all day, do you realize that your eyes will be tired before the rest of your body gets tired and you'll fall asleep earlier than usual and you'll miss time to play with other things?

GENERAL

- You already know that we have to remain clean and presentable when we're having dinner at someone's house, right?
- Do we have messy play in our dress clothes?
- How do we store our dirty-play items?
- Can you please show me what clothes you've put on before going out to splash in puddles?!
- What do we use to clean our noses?
- Do you know where the tissues are?
- What do you need in the garbage?
- Do we play with garbage?

- Do you think we'll be able to put a video in the VCR if something else is occupying the same space – do you think the video will still fit inside, especially if something is stuck in there?
- You know you can tell me if you are upset, right? Can you please also tell me what you'd like to do to get settled? Do you want to play with some cotton wadding or clay?
- You understand that it is rather late in the day to go somewhere for an activity? –But you can start a new messy play activity at home, do you want to take a bath early so that you have more bath playing time? / Make some pudding or gelatin? / Make some dough/homemade noodles?

THE HOW AND WHY OF COGNITIVELY CORRECT

1. Kids should be supervised when playing in snow and should never play around snow removal equipment.
2. Supervise children when they are playing around leaf piles, stick to running through instead of rolling around in them.
3. These answers are meant as improvisation, appealing to the openness, curiosity and intellectual level of children or as creative input for your own ideas   There will be plenty of time for them to learn the scientific explanations, but if you prefer them to understand the universe realistically, you can always visit your local library.

THE HOW AND WHY OF COGNITIVELY INCORRECT

1. If you are worried about dangerous snow activities, especially in areas where snowfall is heavy, get them involved in shoveling or involve yourself in their play activities.
2. Anything your Child feels inclined to explore on their terms that are for a specific purpose would be better left out of their

reach.

3.   For fun and discovery, create a "moon journal" or calendar. Start on the first day of the month, write the name of the moon's phase; crescent, quarter, half, full, etc., or create your own names. Have children draw a picture of the moon's shape. Compare beginning and middle and end of month.

USEFUL MATERIALS / SUPPLIES CHECKLIST

✓ Kaleidoscope

✓ Binoculars

✓ Mini-viewer with photo-slides

✓ Scented oils (with supervision)

✓ Textured materials from nature.

✓ Nature-viewing containers

✓ Nature hikes for 5 senses – seeing, smelling, touching, feeling, hearing/listening

✓ Planting seeds / beans

✓ Children's garden and messy playing tools

✓ Cooking ingredients for exploration –garlic, herbs, (fresh and dry)

✓ Homemade fishing poles – short, stout branch with fishing twine (supervised activity)

✓ Picnic by a waterfall.

✓ Make –draw and color pictures of poisonous bugs and mushrooms (Add names, discuss qualities)

✓ Disposable camera for taking photos of nature creations or discovered items

✓ Children's swimming goggles for snow, leaf and dirt play.

✓ *Autumn Craft Activity - from your collected leaves; decorating a plant box / making collages / a leaf wreath made on donut-shaped cardboard / tape on window-panes, etc.

XIX

SOCIAL FAMILY GUIDANCE

XIX SOCIAL FAMILY GUIDANCE	
Cognitively-Correct[tm]:	*Cognitively-incorrect:*
Please refrain from speaking to me in that tone of voice and take a minute to think about what you really want to tell me.	Don't you dare speak to me in that tone of voice young lady.
You're free to feel any attitude you want, however, I will listen to what you want to say when you're ready to express yourself with some dignity and a respectful tone of voice. (z) If what you have to say is so urgent, let's figure out what you really need/want.	Don't give me that attitude. (z) That's no way to talk to me, I never brought you up to talk that way.[1]

XIX SOCIAL FAMILY GUIDANCE

Cognitively-Correct[m]:	Cognitively-incorrect:
If you'd like your feelings or opinions to be understood or accepted, you have to express them clearly and respectfully. (z) Let me help you find words that express exactly what you mean to say. (y) Please play on your own for a while, when you're ready to show your social manners, then you can join everyone else. (x) If you need to, we'll talk and I'll listen to everything you want to tell me, maybe you'll have something new or different to talk about.[1]	You better show some respect, don't be so rude. We don't talk like that, if you don't have something nice to say, then just keep your mouth shut.[2]
We have set a tradition about candy and we are going to abide by it.	No, we're not buying any candy today, don't ask again. (z) Don't bother me again, or I'll never get you another thing as long as you live.
Please put that back and ask permission before you touch anything. If it happens again, we will leave. (z) That belongs to someone else, we've gone over this rule. (y) I've helped you many times by asking for you, but it's time to ask by yourself now – give it a try.	I told you not to touch things that aren't yours. (z) Just behave yourself and don't touch a thing. (y)If you touch that again, I'm going to smack you. (x) Don't even think about it. (w) No, I'm not asking for you, do your own asking.

XIX SOCIAL FAMILY GUIDANCE

Cognitively-Correct[tm]:	Cognitively-incorrect:
You're entitled to your own feelings and attitudes, however when you express yourself to others that way, there's never going to be a guarantee that they will listen to you. Also it's more difficult to say what you really mean when you're just feeling – it's better to take a minute to talk to yourself first and then talk to the person who upset you. (z) You're allowed to be mad/ feel upset but we talk about it. We never break people's personal things or hurt others or their feelings.	Don't be nasty. (z) You're being very fresh, nobody likes a fresh little boy. (y) Okay, that's it – you're punished, go to your room. (x) You won't be getting any new toys for a while, you've been a very bad boy.
We're having quiet time now, after you play quietly or rest/relax for a little while, we will go out for a treat. I'll put the timer on so you know when your quiet time is over.	If you don't leave me alone so that I can get some work done, we won't go to the park or anywhere, so you better shape up right now.

XIX SOCIAL FAMILY GUIDANCE	
Cognitively-Correct™:	*Cognitively-incorrect:*
I know it's hard to remember the rules when we're upset, but we still have to talk as calmly as possible so that we understand one another. That way I can help you with what you need. (z) I understand that you want everything, but we only get what we *need* and we receive things we **want** for special occasions or days that are designated for treats. (y) You are entitled to cry if you're upset, but you'll have to stop yelling. (x) If you really need to yell, let's go outside and get some fresh air, you are free to yell outside all you like.	You better calm down and stop yelling, or I'll give you something to yell about. (z) If you keep yelling like that, I'm gonna whack you so hard, you won't know what hit you. (y) If you think you can have whatever you want by yelling, you're dead wrong, you may as well shut up, cause you're not getting a thing. (x) That's it, you're being a spoiled brat, just cause you can't have whatever you want, keep it up and you won't get anything for Christmas either.
I have to finish doing one or two things, let's have a look at the clock, when the big hand reaches this number 12 right here, that's when it's time to leave and go to the park. If you let me have five minutes of alone –time, maybe we can go to the park five minutes sooner.	Hey, I don't bother you when you're playing, so don't bother me, how am I supposed to get anything done with you bugging me every minute?
Please tell me the words we use when other people are having a conversation and you would like to say something.	Don't interrupt. (z) Stop being so rude, I've told you a thousand times to mind your manners, stop being a pest.

XIX SOCIAL FAMILY GUIDANCE	
Cognitively-Correct[m]:	**Cognitively-incorrect:**
That's exactly what you should have done, thank you for putting so much effort into it. (z) Thanks for remembering to fulfill your responsibilities (put your toys away, wash your hands, etc.) I'm very proud of you, I hope you're proud of yourself too.[2]	It's about time, what do you want a prize or something – that is what you're supposed to do. You can't expect something special every time you do something you're supposed to do, it's not a special accomplishment you know. (z) What do you want? – special attention for doing something you were supposed to get done two hours ago, I'm not running a praise camp here!
Are you upset about having too little time at the carnival? I can understand that you feel that way. Tomorrow is another day and we'll have some other fun things to do. Are you pouting because you mean to tell me that you are unhappy with this activity or this decision?	Don't be upset (z) Don't pout. Do you think that every time you whine, you'll get what you want? --It doesn't work that way. (z) If you keep pouting/whining like that you won't get anything, as soon as we get home, you'll go to your room, and you can forget about watching your favorite show.[3]
Please sit down while you drink this so you can enjoy every drop, this is all we have. (z) If you want to pour it yourself, I'll put some in a small pitcher.	Don't spill it. (z) Watch out, be careful, if you spill it, there's no more (y) I told you to be careful, there's no more, now you have to learn your lesson the hard way. I'll do it for you.[4]

XIX SOCIAL FAMILY GUIDANCE	
Cognitively-Correct[tm]:	*Cognitively-incorrect:*
Please choose a place to sit so you can enjoy your lollipop. We always sit when we eat anything. If we drop food on the floor, it has to be thrown it away, it's the same with the lollipop, so hold onto it tightly.	Don't run around with that lollipop, if you drop it, that's the end of it, you're not getting another one. (z) I told you to stay still and not run around with the lollipop, now it's dirty, that's it, you're not getting another one.
Please put that snack back. Ask me first, that's the rule about snacks after dinner. (z) The rule about eating snacks after dinner is that it should be a fruit ~you have to have eaten all of your dinner, etc.[3]	You can't have snacks after dinner, you didn't even eat all of your food, if you were hungry you should've eaten all of your dinner.[5]
Look at the clock it's 7:30 already. You can either go upstairs now, brush your teeth, put on your pajamas and then come back to play for 15 more minutes, and have **two** stories before bedtime. −*Or,* you can continue to play for 15 minutes, brush your teeth, put on your P.J's and have just **one** story before bedtime, which do you prefer?[4]	It's time for bed, let's go! (z) No, you can't stay up late, it's your bedtime. (y) You have to go to bed right now, it's already past your bedtime (x) I don't want to hear any whining, I already let you stay up way past your bedtime, let's go!
Could you / would you -like to tell me something about your play date / your day at nursery school? (z)Did you take turns or play alone?	Did you share today? Did you play nice with the other kids at school?
Could you please tell me how you are feeling? − Are you sad? Do you have a stomachache? Do you feel bored / lonely / tired?	What's the matter with you? (z) You've wasted half the day just sitting around doing nothing, find something to do.

XIX SOCIAL FAMILY GUIDANCE

Cognitively-Correct[tm]:	Cognitively-incorrect:
Thanks for trying. (z) Next time you'll be able to try harder, will you promise to put more effort into it next time? (y) I'd like you to put a little more effort into it. (x) Try it a different way for a little while. (w) You did well, now you know you can do it, next time you'll be able to do more/better.[5]	You just didn't try hard enough. I'm very disappointed in you - you could have done better than that. (z) If you don't try hard enough, how do you expect me to give you any rewards?[6]
Can you please repeat what I just told you so that I know you are listening and understand?[6]	Do you understand what I've just told you? (z) If you don't do exactly what I'm telling you, you are going to get the longest time out of your life. (y) If you do that again, I will take one of your privileges away for a really long time.
I need a little time alone to finish this paperwork. —Would you like to read or do some coloring, you can sit next to me and keep me company while I finish this. Or would you prefer to play for 5 minutes on your own?	Don't bother me / Stop bothering me. (z) Leave me alone for a while. Don't bother your little brother, he's sleeping.

XIX SOCIAL FAMILY GUIDANCE

Cognitively-Correct[tm]:	Cognitively-incorrect:
Dinnertime is family time, if you are feeling less hungry than usual, you can still spend this time with us. I'll keep your dinner aside, if you are hungry later, I'll warm it for you. (z) You can eat your dinner now and have a snack later, or you can just eat your dinner later.[7]	If you don't eat your dinner, you can leave the table and get ready for bed right now, you don't think I know what you are trying to do?! (z) You think you can eat junk food all day and then come home and expect not to eat any of your dinner? (y) If you just eat junk food and you don't eat food that's good for you, you won't grow and you'll be sickly.
Let's take a walk outside together for a little while. Whatever the weather is like, it's always a good idea to get some sunlight and fresh air. We get vitamins from the sun that helps our bodies fight sickness so that we can grow strong and healthy.	You can't just stay inside all the time, if you don't get any sun you'll become pale and sick. (z) If you don't go out and get some sun, you'll be white as a ghost. (z) I don't want you staying inside all the time, it's not good for you.
The sooner you get up, the easier it is to be on time to school. (z) I know mornings are difficult – just sit up and relax for a few minutes and then have something to eat. I'll put some soft music on for you.[8]	If you don't get up right away, you'll be late for school / playdate. (z) Snap out of it, what's the matter with you, you think you can sleep your life away, it's the same thing with you every morning. You're going to turn into a lazy bum if you continue with that routine the rest of your life. (y) If you dilly-dally and procrastinate all morning, you'll waste your whole day.

XIX SOCIAL FAMILY GUIDANCE

Cognitively-Correct[tm]:	Cognitively-incorrect:
If falling asleep right now seems impossible or boring, then just sit quietly and look at a few books, everyone has to have some quiet and relaxation time. (z) I know you are feeling quite awake yet, just sit on your bed and read a book, or look out the window and count the stars in the sky, tomorrow morning during breakfast, you can tell me how many there are – if you like.	You'll be a wreck later. You have to take a nap, go to sleep right now. I don't care if you aren't tired yet. You have to go to sleep. (z) I don't want to hear another peep out of you. You just better close your eyes and go to sleep right now. If you don't go to sleep right now, you can forget about going anywhere tomorrow.
Let me hear you whisper![9] We speak in quiet voices inside, especially while the baby is sleeping. –Very good, that's the tone of voice we use inside. If you find it really difficult right now to make less noise, I'll choose an activity for you. Or would you rather choose one by yourself? If you need to make that much noise, please go outside/ down-stairs in the basement.[10]	Don't yell like that, we don't live in a baseball stadium you know. (z) If you keep yelling like that, I'll put a sock in your mouth. (y) You're giving me a headache. I can't take your yelling anymore.(x) If you yell once more, you'll spend the rest of your day in your room. (w) If I have to listen to you scream once more, I don't know what I'm going to do.
You have 10 more minutes to watch T.V. before you figure out what else to do. If you need help, I'll be glad to offer you some ideas.	Turn off the T.V. and go find something else to do, your brain cells are going to get fried. (z) If you just watch T.V. all day, you'll turn into an air-head / space-cadet / mummy.

COMMENTS AS QUESTIONS

MANNERS & SOCIAL AWARENESS

- Is that the way we speak to one another?
- Do you remember the phrase we use when we have something to say when someone else is having a conversation?
- Do you want to stay here and play or do you want to leave?
- Are you going to take turns with your friends or play by yourself?
- If you have a disagreement with one of your friends will you do your best to tell the teacher?
- Did you have an enjoyable day at school?

CONSIDERATION

- Do we touch other people's things without permission? Is that yours?
- If you are unsure about something, will you promise to ask the teacher?
- Would you like to tell me something about why you are so upset?
- I'm sorry you're disappointed because you lost your turn with that toy / activity. Would you like me to speak to your teacher tomorrow?
- Do you really think your brother wants to be bothered – did you take time to tell him what you really want – to play with him / to go outside together, etc?
- Can we figure out a way for both of you to be happy with that toy, can we take turns?

CAUSE & EFFECT GENERAL

- Is that candy going to be just for you or are going to offer some to a friend?
- Would you like me to write that on paper for you so that you can remind me tomorrow?
- Do we yell inside or outside?
- I have an idea, would you like to have some extra time at the park today? -Okay, however long you play very quietly here before we leave, that's how much longer we'll stay at the park. Let's have a look at the clock, would you like to start right now?
- Would you like a sticker on your chart for getting that done?
- Do you know what you are going to do at school today?
- For every 5 minutes you play quietly, you can have an extra bedtime story tonight, would you like that?
- What do you think will happen if that lollipop falls on the ground?
- How many lollipops do you see me holding? Correct, only one, so please hold on tightly and sit down while you enjoy it, okay?
- What do you think will happen if the milk spills?
- Have you had a look at the clock?
- What do you think will happen if you go to sleep later / stay up late?
- Do you think you could have tried much harder?
- How soon do you want to go out for ice cream? Well the quieter you are, the sooner we'll go out, we all need 10 minutes of quiet time, can you help me with that?
- Do you want to have 2 stories before bedtime or 3 stories before bedtime? Okay, if you brush your teeth now that we're done

with dinner and dessert, you can have 3 stories later, if you wait until 8 o'clock then you can have just two stories, which do you prefer?

THE HOW AND WHY OF
THE COGNITIVELY CORRECT

1. Avoid giving too much time, credit or attention to disrespect or negative expressions, after all- does it warrant your energy as much as your Child's need for guidance? –Ask questions, look into the real reason or motive, for instance, they heard someone else say it. Then re-direct their expression, giving attention to their right to express and do so with integrity. Help them with optional words or phrases, have them repeat what you say, follow the same routine until children become accustomed to re-structured- various expressions. Judgment produces nothing except feeling of shame. Children must feel free to express themselves, and guidance that defines all possible expressions helps children become responsible for what they say and develop the capability to say what they think and feel.

2. Doing what they're "supposed" to do is still new to them, they have so little experience with habits and/or daily chores. They need encouragement to develop that sense of competency and regularity that adults have for maintaining things that are "supposed to be done". If you make a big deal about what they've done wrong, and never a big deal about what they do right, you miss the opportunity to help them develop a **desire** to do the right thing.. What's more, if you can give that much attention to what they do wrong, what's wrong with giving them attention for what they do right?

3. When implementing new rules, remember to help solidify new habits by having them retrace their steps- or post it in writing.

4. —Or, jumble it whichever way is going to get both you and your

Child at a vantage point that is desirable for both of you. The requisite for cooperation here is that **all transitions** should be given a time element warning. In addition, conjoining as many diversified elements of their learning functions as possible is the best way to entice and encourage the 'preschooler' while giving credit to their developing intellect.

5.   If your Child is still becoming accustomed to a new task or activity on their own - offer praise for their efforts.

6.   You can start the sentence and let them finish it, or have them repeat with you, either way they will have said the words themselves which means that they can do little to block it out. It rules out selective hearing, because you have elected them to talk to themselves. Example: "Pulling on my sister's hair hurts her. I promise to treat my sister with gentleness, love and kindness. If I want to pull on something I will go outside and pull my little red wagon around for a while."

7.   This should let them know ahead of time if they are dodging dinner now to try and replace it later with a snack, that their options are already set. There are times to expose their motives in more serious situations, in many cases you only have to offer the options.

8.   The morning transition is just as useful as the evening transition. By now you will have figured out if your Child is a "morning person'" or a "night person". If you are the opposite of your Child and try to make their temperament fit yours, chances are you'll create an uncooperative friction between you; an unnecessary and easily avoidable friction. If your Child is the type to burn the candle at both ends, take heart, it is usually a sign of above average intelligence.

9.   Have them say it with you while you whisper yourself.

10.   Children should have some space and time to get some noisy play done on a daily basis, it's part of their development requirements, it can be classified as a cognitive ability; learning contrasts.

THE HOW AND WHY OF
THE COGNITIVELY INCORRECT

1. Try to keep in mind that they are testing limits with speech and rules and other expectations, it's rarely ever personal toward you, deal with it as a development issue.

2. Acts of disrespect, aggression, or defiance are symptoms – symptoms are indications of a problem or challenge, but are often treated as the problem itself. The actual problems or causes can range from ~ newly, discovered feelings to totally or partially unresolved feelings. These behaviors can also demonstrate their desire to test others reactions, or it can simply be a new impulse manifesting from an ability that is unrefined, because it is just beginning to surface. Fueling an attitude war just fans fire to the symptoms. It may seem reasonable and logical to deal with undesirable symptoms, but would you try to prevent a Child from laughing because he is happy? If you want acts of disrespect and aggression to disappear, deal with the causes and issues. If you want them to keep laughing– find out what's so funny, it works both ways

3. Keep in mind that one thing has nothing to do with another. Whatever the reason they are going without, that is enough punishment. Their reward is learning to deal with disappointment, give them credit for that.

4. Very few children have expertise in anything. If you criticize, and put them to shame, then their ability to feel competent is undermined. If they spill something, let them clean it up with the same effort as whatever they tried to do beforehand. These two tasks that adults classify as separate are really one continuing flow of activity for preschool age children. It follows the conglomerate of diversified learning.

5. Make the criteria clear first – if the entire portion of dinner is finished, then they could have a snack later.

6. Only genuine encouragement works for building confidence, faith and trust. Saying nothing, at all, or missing out on a chance to do some "coaching" when the going gets a little rough, will yield sluggish attitudes and little fortification for children to connect with their capabilities. Your belief in them should be their reward.

USEFUL MATERIALS / SUPPLIES CHECKLIST

✓ Timer (for taking turns)

✓ Reward / Accomplishment chart

✓ Miniature carrying notebook & pencil

✓ Small pitchers (for pouring)

✓ Small brooms (for cleaning)

✓ Pre-talk for all events and activities (with the expectation that they *will* do certain things. Pre-talks should exclude expressing discontent, and complicated negative directions foreboding all the wrong things. Pre-talks should anticipate contentment and harmony.)

APPENDIX C

A note about Guidance ~

Guidance is a very sensitive area that is tempered by individual viewpoints, experience, observation, knowledge, upbringing, personal issues, culture, peer influence, and the subjective themes of any given generation. The question to ask yourself regarding guidance is if your objective is to actually *punish* children? Or is it to help them/ guide them/develop in them, a desire to do the right thing and create virtuous habits that will be beneficial to their lives and to that of others. Problem solving, honest confidence, and encouragement toward respective individual potentials is the best guidance a parent can offer a Child for a life of quality, compassion and independence. So, for instance, if in your home you have a rule that basketball can be played *inside* the house when it is raining *outside,* then it would be wise to incorporate rules consistent with an overall regard for appropriate living conditions as well.

The connections for diversified learning functions for pre-school age children demand logical consistence through flexibility as well as limitations for safety and respect for the environment. Guidance is as individualized for the Child receiving it as the adult administering it. It should be personalized and creative while it intentionally upholds the basic requirements for early Childhood growth and development.

CHAPTER XX

CONCLUSION

We have the ability to express both abstract and literal ideas. So what if we communicate messages that actually equal the literal or abstract ideas we intend on expressing?

If we start out pure, innocent and good without speaking words, but end up speaking in maladies and negations, is there a possibility for considering that language can be adjusted so that we maintain as much of the appreciable goodness that nature intended for us and included in our design?

When children are young, they feel compelled to do whatever their impulses direct them to do. Ultimately, the day comes when they stop skipping down the street while talking to imaginary people. In the beginning of our lives, we look forward to the possibilities of enjoyment and fulfillment. Although we consider ourselves to "grow-up" and include other's feelings and opinions, we're deceptively cultivated to submit to status quo expectations. That means that rather than view each and every person with compassionate value and creative and productive abilities, we worry too much about their social opinions of us.

So what happens when we retire to the ends of our lives? Towards the end, we look back and reflect on the dreams we were willing to challenge, the ones we left to chance, the ones we kept hidden from the rest of the world and sadly even from ourselves. It is a common misunderstanding that people look back on their lives with regret for their misdeeds, but it is the missed dreams and lost chances for greatness that fill our hearts with despair. When the labor of life is over, we worry about what the fruits of our labors have amounted to, and then we wonder why we had subscribed to a program of lesser expectations and incompleteness.

When people reach their senior years they wonder how and why they ever started worrying too much about everyone else's agenda for *their* lives. It happens when we give up our own desires and have adopted the knowledge of guilt as our own emotional law to live by. At that point, the wish is to go back in time and look ahead to the future once again without wanting or waiting for the approval of others. The lamentation of lost personal ideals becomes a decidedly unwelcome mood when we realize we could have pursued our dreams - followed our hearts. Instead, we followed conventional standards and rejected our own hearts' real desires and inclinations.

Everyone is responsible for what they know. We all possess an inherent design for moral fortitude. Although children instinctively understand the differences between right and wrong, it is an adult's responsibility to continually indulge them with encouraging guidance and experiences that solidify their abilities to be intellectually and emotionally competent decision-makers. Children's abilities have to be indulged so they can acquire the tenacity to follow their hearts which are valid indicators about their talents and potentials.

What do we owe ourselves? What do we owe children? Are there any guarantees that we will escape tribulations and tragedy or inversely, experience all the wonderful things life has to offer? Neither is guaranteed! Is comfort and security gained by how many precautions we take, or by how many risks we're willing to go after? Do we derive more peace and serenity from knowing the disadvantages in any given situation or, do we stand to warrant more from knowing what the advantages are in any given situation?   The call for positive terminology skills is a deliberate attempt to re-design, re-create and reverse debilitating communication so that our good intentions can flourish without the interference of negative messages, connotations and implications that turn every idea into an immediate problem. It also establishes a provision for speaking with children whereby the personal issues of adults can be omitted from conversations and expectations, because "cognitively-correct^{tm}" speech means children's developmental needs are being addressed. Positive guidance calls us to speak to the particular abilities in each Child, rather then from the fears of our own inhibitions and limitations.

Our emotions are our call to action. When we are feeling good and understood we feel capable of doing and saying what is expected of us personally, socially and professionally. But when we have difficult challenges or experience flashes of anger, what then are we capable of and what are acceptable forms of expressions? How odd it is that we implore one another to remain cool, stay calm or be rational and reasonable in moments of uncertainty and difficulty? Most of our language expressions convince us to view ourselves and our circumstances by a measure of disadvantages and consequences. Why suddenly then do we feel obligated to convince one another that we should be positive during moments of justifiable distress?!

If we expect to feel and think rationally and positively when we are angered or disturbed, we are certainly going to have to make a case against ourselves for seeing the positive and rational possibilities when we are feeling "normal" Our truly "normal" design and natural disposition is for usefulness and fulfillment. Therefore our language semantics should be characteristics of trust, competence and possibilities cultivating a dialect that promotes a knowledge of potential.

The truth is if we were normally inclined to speak according to the benefits and advantages of our daily circumstances, it would naturally be easier to perceive for ourselves the advantages and solutions of our distressed reactions. We would have that as a regular frame of reference. If we expect to be positive and rational when we're feeling upset, angry or distressed, we are certainly going to have to raise the bar of feeling positive during the times we are supposedly feeling normal.

Consider dedicating a day or even just a couple of hours to record some conversations with a Child, a co-worker, or a friend. Transcribe your conversation, and split it into two sections side by side. On one side, list the verbs you negate, the inabilities you propose in yourself and in others, the disadvantages or consequences of a situation, and any other type of negative judgments you assume. In the second, or opposite section, record your positive expectations, any abilities and good attributes you recognize about yourself and others, and any plans you vouch, create or anticipate to include constructive action and changes (reflecting advantages and benefits). Make a study of how your speech and attitudes reflect the "knowledge of disadvantages, guilt and impossibilities" vs. the "Knowledge of Potential and Benefits".

Generation after generation, children are born reflecting the ultimate ideals of human nature. However unrefined their impulses may be, children represent the purity and innocence of goodwill, unconditional trust, love and the freedom to just be themselves. We have all been in the shoes of a child, experiencing all the sentiments that a child experiences. Whether we come from happy or humble origins, inside each of us, there is still a Child waiting to be recognized, liberated and given a chance to be altruistic heroes of our own destinies.

The theory behind positive terminology and development emerges as a needed inoculation against a virus of negative attitudes, and beliefs. Its purpose and function is to filter the purity of our "desire-able" aptitudes, and to propose a legacy of positive ability from birth that matches all of our intentions for fulfillment.

Early education caretakers need to address more than just the omission of negations or children's inability to hypothesize constructive options on their own. We need to raise the consciousness of our communication skills from the "knowledge of consequences and disadvantages" to the "knowledge of potential and possibilities".

Preschool age children are experiencing a special stage wherein all foundations for lifetime learning and development are being established. This challenge can be done with cognitively-correct[tm] guidance and responses that meet the requirements for natural human nature, coordinating emotional intelligence (I.Q.) and intellectual intelligence (E.Q.) as one complimentary function.

Once you discover how incredibly brilliant, trusting, attractive and able this stage is, you'll be smitten with delight. Enjoy them and yourself.

Thank you.

THE END

For more information on Seminars or other
"Connecting the Dots" Resources
Please visit www.ccthedots.com

BIBLIOGRAPHY / SUGGESTED READING

This work was compiled predominantly through observations and experiences with children of all ages but most especially with preschool children in accordance with that learned under my mentor Laura Jean Gilfillan and Professor Lauretta Freeman, MA of Montclair State University, Montclair, New Jersey.

PRIMARY BIBLIOGRAPHICAL SOURCE –National CDA certification course work files and evidence under Prof. Lauretta Freeman.

The following texts are in their entireties both Bibliography and suggested reading:

Emotional Intelligence By Daniel Goleman

Children: The Challenge By Rudolph Dreikurs with Vicki Stolz

Raising Kids – How Does Your Child Learn? By Thomas Hoerr Ph.d

A Different Kind of Classroom – Teaching with Dimensions of Learning By Robert J. Marzano

Sheparding a Child's Heart By Tedd Tripp

Raising Caine by Dan Kindlon and Michael Thompson

The Birth of Pleasure – a New Map of Love By Carol Gilligan

Longing for Dad – Father Loss and Its Impact By Beth M. Erickson

Literacy Development in the Early Years By Lesley Mandel Morro

What's Going on in There? How the Brain Develops in the First Five Years of Life By Lise Eliot

How to Help Children with Common Problems By Charles E. Schaefer, Howard L. Millman

Art of Young Children By Jane Cooper Bland

Love Must Be Tough By James C. Dobson

Psycho-Cybernetics By Maxwell Maltz, M.D., F.I.C.S.

Stupid Things Parents Do To Mess Up Their Kids By Dr. Laura Schlessinger

Getting the Love You Want: A Guide for Couples By Dr. Harville Hendrix

GLOSSARY / INDEX
TRUE DEFINITIONS BASED ON HUMAN DESIGN

A

Abilities - Natural capacity to perform certain tasks, activities or crafts.

Achievement - Successful completion of a goal, task, activity or feeling of satisfaction.

Acquisition - A merge, union or acceptance with an idea, image or object.

Advantages - A benefit or an element of usefulness.

Appropriate/Appropriately - An application that favorably matches a situation. A clinical or precise plan that secures and supports a basic design or completes a program for development or progress.

Aptitude - An ability or a significantly strong clue or sign of a particular talent.

Attitude - Combined ideas and feelings together that reveal or support opinions and motives.

B

Bad - Behavior that is judged as unacceptable and undesirable but usually preventable in young children's impulses by observing natural inclinations and enforcing activities that match unique abilities.

Behavior - Actions, reactions and interactions. Actions and habits that reveal feelings, ideas and impulses. Actions that can be enforced with cognitively-correct[tm] guidance.

Belief, Believe - A strong sense or idea that someone or something is worthy. A feeling for something, for oneself or for someone else. An attitude that supports an idea.

Blame - Withholding responsibility or control for actions, intentions or destiny. Feeling that someone or something else is in control.

Blueprint - A basic template or prototype that is designed to be imprinted with something. A basic blank form ready to be structured or drawn upon to create a unique set of details.

C

Catalyst - An aid, element or chemical that enhances or speeds up a process.

Challenge - An act or attempt to do something or achieve something that is unusual, different or more difficult than expected. The intention to seek and apply a solution to a problematic situation.

Characteristics - The unique or particular aspects or attributes of an object, person or situation that define personality or specific effects. Childhood - the time or period of life that classifies the early years and stages of development, learning and growth. The human qualities of innocence or a period of time of pure thought and palpable ability to absorb new information rapidly and with a greater propensity for retaining it.

Childhood -The time or period of life that classifies the early years and stages of development, learning and growth. The human qualities of innocence, pure thought and palpable ability to absorb new information rapidly with as profound a propensity for retaining it. The growth stages of certain developments that must be addressed with particular requisites for appropriate cognitive development. The time of preschool development when a Child's job is to play and learn through playing.

Classification - An order of group of qualities that share similarities or common characteristics. One of the fundamental principles of preschool math also referred to as 'cognitive development'.

Cognition - In nature; a pattern, order and sequence of information that represents instinctive knowledge or purpose. In human development, cognition represents and defines all functions of learning which are dependant on simple and interconnected patterns. This process simultaneously defines early math learning and the basis for all subjects of learning which have their origin in fundamental math. Cognition is a two-fold intertwined process in human development. Since cognition means our ability to absorb information and gain knowledge through all of the senses and since all subjects are fundamentally mathematical then cognition is the practice and progress of basic math. In simple terms *cognition is the basic principles of math at work for acquiring logical knowledge.*

Cognitively-Correct[tm] - The logical mathematical process of inputting information and knowledge into our two main intelligence quotients.

Communication - The ways we express or convey our heart, mind, body and soul. The basis for language, bonding, interaction and relationships. Communication may be expressed orally and through non-oral, but literal verb or action forms such as and including lyrics, sign language, music, poetry, art, dance, books, acting and everyday behavior.

Compassion - Inherently knowing, feeling and understanding the value of oneself and being able to extend that sense of value to others. The substantially active link between the Emotional Intelligence Quotient (E.Q.) and the Intellectual Intelligence Quotient (I.Q.). The objective or subjective quality and intention to create solutions and harmony by sensing, and developing an understanding of another's position.

Competence - A second-nature impulse, disciplined compulsion or managed habit to fulfill and complete tasks and activities either through desire or responsibility.

Complementary - An element or act that devotes or adds approval to another act or element. An equal but different cause or effect - an interlocking element or idea that completes a substance.

Composition - The make-up, substance and characteristics of an element or entity whether living or non-living.

Compulsion - An involuntary or almost involuntary impulse to do, be, act, or react based on nature, instinct, desire, need, ability, aptitude, talent or attitude.

Conflict - A cause, effect, characteristic, action or communication that repels, opposes or contradicts another effect.

Conjunction - A position, substance, element or part of speech that connects two or more other key components.

Connection - An entity, notion, subject, idea or substance that joins two or more separate formations whether abstract or realistic and concrete.

Consequences - The results of a circumstance or event that are usually considered undesirable or unfavorable.

Constructive - The finality, result or process of structuring or putting something together through planning, time and effort. Creating something with purpose and usefulness.

Contempt - A strong perception or substantial feeling of dislike, repulsion or hatred generally directed toward something or someone. A form of dislike or hatred often fueled by resentment, envy or misunderstanding. A total misunderstanding based on unjust, pre-judged or harsh criticism. A feeling that fills the senses with the pain of unfulfilled dreams.

Contrast - An attribute often classified alongside with, or similar to 'conflict', but in fact displays a varying effect by enhancing another element, idea, component or situation.

Conviction - A sense of determination compelled by a variety of motives and experiences.

Cooperation - An act or intention of merging with a group, individual or authority for the purpose of developing harmony, unity or social esteem and order.

Critical-thinking skills - The ability to put intuitive knowledge to work. The practice of adding logical and correlating elements and principles to a situation or challenge.

Cultivate - Acquiring or inviting certain aspects or steps that will help to develop a likeness or acceptance. Contributing certain efforts an aspects toward something in order to solicit its growth, development or result.

D

Debilitate - Cutting off or diminishing an ability, condition, or attribute that would otherwise be helpful, useful, or fulfilling.

Deception - The face or masquerade of something presenting itself as something entirely different than its real internal characteristics. The ability of an idea or someone to completely divert an issue, purpose or intention with such perfection that its underlying agenda is undetectable. An unrecognizable flaw that recycles useless and destructive practices under the auspice of good intentions.

Design - A simple pattern or substance that functions as a basic template for a more complex system or program to be implemented. A completed pattern. A product with a specific function or essence that requires a matching program for full functionality.

Destructive - The complete conflicting and opposing effect of what would be constructive. The cause of annihilation. To destroy or belittle something or someone so as to cause partial or total dysfunction.

Development - The emerging characteristics of movement growth, advancement, change or structure of a person, innovation or creation.

Dialect - A type of language. A language within a language. The manner or characterization of a group of people creating and developing an identity withing their own culture or language to communicate based on special circumstances, immediate environment or certain social priorities.

Disadvantages - The lack of benefits. The negative or undesirable outcomes of a situation, belief or action.

Discipline - The conventional understanding that acts of misbehavior must be rehabilitated or that time and energy must be utilized to purge the body and soul of unfavorable habits or poor motives. The true understanding that discipline is actually a term referring to advanced or refined skills in a particular field or endeavor and therefore referred to as 'a discipline.' The practical matter of contributing time and energy into constructing talents so that discipline never or rarely has to be wasted merely on the avoidance of bad behavior or useless habits.

Discover - The experience of revelation or witnessing something new. The process of learning about the patterns and elements of an interconnecting universe.

Diversify/Diversification - The setting, availability and practice of interjecting as many varied functions and elements as possible for learning so as to exercise both the E.Q. and I.Q.

DNA - The basic design of cellular life. The pattern in each seed of a life form that contains all the information for its formation and growth. The genetic codes or inherited traits for a new life. A basic blueprint for unique forms of life that determine its structure, form and classification in the cycles of living things.

E

Early Education - The first formal introduction to learning. The organized setting, whether familial, social, religious or political that are obligated to provide opportunities and activities that meet the requisites and requirements of growth and early human development according to the natural cognitive design of human life. The stage of education and development that includes the process of learning about the interconnected natural world with diversified activities. The time of life where discovery and exploration can offer clues about an individual's unique talents and abilities.

Education - Learning and gaining knowledge through formal instruction or institutions and programs. Learning valuable studies and disciplines throughout life via vocations, self-taught skills, extensive reading, observations, apprenticeship and research.

Elements - A simple single ingredient with its own value and characteristics of nature. The compiled formations that make up the substance of the world and universe.

Emotion/Emotional - Anything that pertains to feelings or processes from the emotional intelligence quotient. The inclinations and drives of desire.

Emotional Cognition - The process of acquiring emotional knowledge. The exploration and discovery of different and distinct emotions. The process of acquiring and developing a literacy in the realm of emotions so as to re-use that knowledge logically, expressively, purposefully and constructively. The definition of respective emotions that contribute to a wealth of emotional knowledge & intelligence.

Emotional Intelligence - The first type of acquired knowledge that contributes to and makes up a major part of our psyche and consciousness, motives, competence and inclinations to interact. (For more on this topic Read Emotional Intelligence by Daniel Goleman).

Enforce/Enforcement - Maintaining structure and order for what has already been put in place. Creating and implementing standards for behavior and surroundings. The complementary counterpart of reinforcement.

E.Q. - Emotional intelligence quotient.

Explore - Knowingly or unknowingly observing, seeking, absorbing and learning facts and information about anything through available resources. The wonder of experiencing the world and the environment and the substances that make up an interconnected world.

F

Force (s) - A bolt or impact of energy. A powerful movement that sets something in motion. The elements that make up the power of enforcement and reinforcement.

G

Good/Goodness - A feeling or sense of that all is well and favorable. The quality of a matter or person that lacks disturbance, disharmony or anything considered bad.

Guidance - Words of wisdom. Specific sensible direction or advice that meets the demands for tasks, challenges, confusion or for creating security and stability.

Guilt - The feeling of being enticed or pushed against one's own will. The sense that personal actions and motives must be re-directed and performed according to someone else's will, intentions or priorities. Relinquishing ownership of feelings, ideas and natural impulses that are imbued during a stage of early development. The inability to confidently hypothesize, theorize, or defend one's own desires, inadvertently becoming "natural" feelings and habits.

H

Heritage - The mark of history that defines itself in groups of people honoring customs, behaviors, habits and identity.

History - The study of the stories of mankind's environment, social habits, standards and habits. The development of culture, languages, nations and their philosophical and political orders and the events that change them. The traditions that mold legacies.

Hypothesize - The ability to see, create, recognize or develop a theory and premise that concludes a truth and yields usefulness. The learned skill of following a pattern or being able to perceive the missing parts of a sequence. The ability to make E.Q. and I.Q. work together harmoniously.

I

Idioms - Insinuations with words. Creative or regional terms that make up colloquialisms. Phrases and words that are unusual or exceptional according to the regular uses of language. Acceptable parts of speech that may be grammatically incorrect in other instances but are consistent with other comparable meanings. Types of phrases that are used to express particular meanings.

Imagination - The keeper of all possibilities. The temple of innovation. The reliable, loyal and dedicated defender of all hopes and dreams. The zone of unlimited feelings and thoughts that are protected and free from all trespassers.

Impossibilities - The notion that possibilities are virtually unattainable. The idea that possibilities can be dismissed. The mind set or attitude that restricts entertaining options and gives support to the "knowledge of disadvantages."

Impulse - An instant reaction almost without thinking. A seemingly unconscious compulsion to act upon a motive or feeling that stems from natural or cultivated inclinations.

Inclinations - Leaning toward an impulse or compulsion to do something. A feeling or sense to act upon an ability or motive. . .

Inherent - A built-in response or design system to lean toward certain behavior.

Intellect/Intellectual - The activity of the brain. The storage of information, facts, knowledge and memories that are combined together and available to use and re-use for social, interactive, educational and personal purposes.

Intentions - The temperament of heart, thought and motive that usually results in an action, attitude or both.

Interconnected - The process or existence whereby several or multiple entities are either directly or indirectly connected.

Intuition/Intuitive - The ability to perceive, see, envision or feel the connection between different attributes, characteristics or situations even though they seem unconnected on the surface or at first glance. Intuition may be part of I.Q. or E.Q., but usually functions by or is powered by both.

I.Q. - Intellectual intelligence quotient.

L

Language - The system of words, phrases and grammatical structure that represents or reflects a group of people and is characteristic of their culture. A way of communicating that is verbal. A system of communication that is usually oral. A venue for expression through which the main parts of speech are verbs -action words- whether oral, bodily or symbolic. The various ways of expression that can be lyrical, musical, kinesthetic or artistic.

Legacy - A type of inheritance that contains attitudes, esteem and a variation of cultural, social, political, familial or personal traits and often expectations. A version of livelihood that can be altered to suit the times and merit of people or persons.

Love - The most widely coveted, longed for, pursued, celebrated and spoken about emotion. The highest order of emotion. The intention of bonding. A favored projection of emotion for someone whether they are present or at a distance. A bond that exceeds the confines of time, space or condition. A bond based on an initial relationship of trust and good intentions. The drive and purpose of human development, growth, survival and reason for living.

M

Malice/Malicious - A feeling or motive that lacks good intentions. The lack of goodness or dignity. An immature characteristic of personality that is usually cultivated through the absence of nurturing love, encouragement or the recognition of desirable abilities. An acquired inclination to do badly by others or to others.

Math/Mathematical - The simple and complex principles that reflect the design, composition and structure of all elements in the universe. The basis for all subjects of learning. The subject classified as "cognitive development" for preschoolers. The functions of exploration that allow preschool children to discover the interconnecting elements of the earth and universe. The connections and links that develop and create the basis for hypothesizing. The function that supports the capacity to build intuition and critical-thinking skills. A refined ability for innovative thinking, solution-seeking and problem solving skills.

Mental - The process and activities of the mind. The use of energy in the mind to use acquired or desired knowledge. A state of mind or a term used to describe a state of mind.

Motives - The motional attitudes, inclinations and impulses that determine reasons for action. The emotional component of trust or mistrust that propels a purpose to act, react and interact.

N

Nature/Natural - The elements of a composition. The attributes that determine a form of life. The parts of life or living things that are virtually absolute. The mathematical process of cause of effect.

Negative - The opposite of positive. One part of polarity and natural life that represents equal value and purpose to positive. A characteristic of life that is designed to contrast positivity without conflicting with it. A definition that is associated with bad or evil consequences with rare respect to any positive influences or advantages.

Negations - The process of minimizing or diminishing a verb. The halting or movement or progress through the reckless or overuse of action words that can easily be replaced by suffixes or prefixes creating an actual verb form.

O

Order - The pattern, sequence or organization of a system. The logical implementation for progress.

Ownership - The premise for teaching and instilling a heart-felt basis for responsibility. The unconditional allowance for full acceptance and recognition of thoughts, feelings and possessions. The freedom and respect to oversee and take care of environment and others. A venue for extending trust that builds confident competency.

P

Patterns - The most fundamental order and blueprint of all functions, living and non-living. The most fundamental principle of math. The numerical layout of a blueprint or template of an any object that has purpose, order or a reproducible effect.

Polarity - An element that has an inverted pattern of another element and is designed to collaborate as a contrasting or interconnecting feature for the purpose of creating something new or whole. The quality of an abstract or concrete entity that has equal value to its complementary object. The complete difference between one quality and another. Qualitative elements with distinctive characteristics that can be fitted together to serve a greater purpose or function.

Positive - A sign, symbol or understanding usually defined by a plus or something good or gained. The natural complement of "negative". The overly zealous idea that positive means the lack of negativity or bad vibrations. An ideal often sought after with the belief that there is a overall presence of peace, goodness and the lack of confrontation. The process whereby a purposeful confrontation can produce a result or string of effects that bring further progress.

Possibilities - The thought and process of entertaining, implementing and innovating ideas and options for a purpose or solution. Acting on advantages, imagination, intuition, trust and competence.

Potential - The basic blueprint, clue, desire or inclination to exhibit and/or pursue certain talents, aptitudes and abilities. The propensity and fundamental evidence for a specific talent. Productive - the actual process or work of a constructive purpose. The process behind achieving a result.

Productive - The actual process or work of an constructive purpose. The process behind achieving a result.

Propose - A presentation or exhibition of an idea or work. The intricate and orderly details of a plan. A simple notion that is innovative. The demonstration of an idea.

Psyche - An aspect of consciousness that records memories, natural or learned reflexes, motives, and desires. The part of being that connects all experiences of mind, body, soul and emotion.

Q

Quotient - The result of a cause. The yield of variables that equal and represent a quality of potential, use or purpose. A number reflecting the total sum of other qualities or numbers.

R

Recognition/Re-cognition, Re-cognize - The re-use of gained knowledge. The feedback of cognitive abilities. A recollection process at work. The ability to manage and re-manage already acquired and newly acquired attitudes, beliefs or knowledge.

Requirement - A demand that may be referred to as an absolute necessity, but could have flexible options.

Requisite - A characteristic of a requirement. A component or part of a requirement. A proper implementation of a quality, speciality or idea that makes something or someone soundly functional.

Responsibility - The growing and consistent maturity to perform tasks and obligations. The acquiring desire to tackle and accomplish activities that are necessary for life, order and recreation. The instance of owning or owning up to the fulfillment of destiny or a contribution to a task, relationship, position, group of people or legacy.

RNA - The motivating force and purpose behind DNA. The catalytic basis that sets DNA in progress. The messenger of DNA that helps produce life. The originating substance of evolutionary formations and the carrier of evolutionary information.

S

Semantics - The workings ~ the clockwork of a language and the structural blueprint for expressing and conveying ideas and intentions. A formula within language that is a commitment to standardize communication with certain precision. The dynamics of a language that reflect the character of its respective culture.

Shame - The product of criticism, judgment, guilt and the absence of compassion. The lack of honor originally conceived through an authoritative assumption that early stage impulses were driven by bad motives or pre-meditated malicious thought. An overly-cultivated emotion that gives prolific energy to the "knowledge of guilt and consequences" and undermines the "knowledge of potential and advantages".

Solution (s) - The liberating quality of engaging a problem or challenge with a remedy or alteration for constructive and purposeful effects and advantages.

Spectrum - A scale demonstrating all possible characteristics of a circumstance or object.

Speech - Verbal presentation, exhibition or demonstration of a language or dialect.

Spiritual - The attributes, characteristics, or senses of a substantial energy usually associated with the fourth, fifth or twelfth dimensions or any dimensions outside of the third dimension. The transference of energy that is felt by emotional and mental senses. An idea or philosophy that priorities and pursuits can be driven by motives and mind sets other than conventional or worldly reasons.

Structure - The skeletal order or formula of an event, activity, creation or plan. An aid of guidance through enforcement.

T

Talents - The unique abilities of an individual that characterize and define personal identity and personality. Special abilities.

Technique - The steps or formula of a design, plan or program. The simple or complex pace, details and sequence that puts an object or idea to work.

Tendency - The feeling, impulse or inclination that someone or something leans toward. The instinct or compulsion to do, go or move in a particular direction.

Traits - Specific clues about talent, personality, character or heritage. The pattern of elements or structural design that have concise or relative factors.

Trust - The fundamental basis for all relationships, live or inanimate. An ongoing interaction that initiates and fuels bonding and intimacy. The portal for love, virtuosity, confidence and competence.

Truth - Facts and information that are indisputable regardless of beliefs or justifications.

FINAL NOTE FROM THE AUTHOR -

Log onto our website for www.ccthedots.com for information about the release of our "Cognitively - Correct[tm] Learning Manual & Workbook". Through "Connecting the Dots" you will have learned how to transform guidance from negative to positive, from purposeless to constructive. In the workbook, we promise to give you a greater understanding and practice of "Cognitively - Correct[tm] language according to the knowledge of potential and benefits.